2016

The America We Live In-A View from 30,000 feet

CLINT VOGUS

ISBN-13: 978-1516964062

ISBN-10: 1516964063

1. The America We Live In-A View From 30,000 feet

About the Author

Clint Vogus is a full-time faculty member at Arkansas State University in the College of Business teaching business management and strategy and a consultant to businesses and non-profit organizations.

He is also the author of a *Current View of Higher Education*.

Prior to his academic career, Clint spent a number of years as a manager, educator, trainer, and change agent in a variety of businesses both in the U.S. and overseas.

He is active in supporting his community as a member of Rotary, Big Brothers and Big Sisters, United Way, and the Single Parent Scholarship Fund. He serves as a board member and volunteer.

His goal is to continue to work to better inform people about the current state of America so that each person can make better informed decisions for themselves and their families.

Contact him at vogusfamily@earthlink.net

Dedication and Thanks

This book is dedicated to those who are seeking a better understanding of the America we now live, and how they can build a better life for themselves, their families, and for future generations.

A very special thanks to Mona Fielder and Virginia Shackelford who not only assisted with the editing for the book, but challenged my thinking to make this book what it has turned out to be. Without them, you would not be reading this book. I will forever be indebted to them both.

Also by Clint Vogus:

A Current View of Higher Eduction-2015

Contents

Chapter 1
Introduction

Having lived a long life, I have a historical perspective from which I can compare today with yesterday. A lot has changed in my life-time; much for the better, some for the worse.

Long before I was born, this place we call America was settled by men and women who were willing to venture into the unknown for the promise of a better life than the one they had.

America and Change
Change can be frightening, as it often pushes us towards the unknown and away from our comfort zone. As Americans we need to remember that our country was born out of change.

America began as a collection of European immigrants seeking a life of freedom and self-determination. People from different religious beliefs, languages, skills, and expectations came together to form communities in the New World. In the settling of the New World, citizens from Spain, France, Holland, and Great Britain came together. Eventually Great Britain became the dominant ruler of the American Colonies, and began treating American Colonists as subservient to their government. As Britain strengthened its control over the American Colonies, many citizens became more resistant to British rule. What the settlers of the American Colonies sought in freedom and self-determination was now being taken from them.

Thomas Paine, in his book, *Common Sense*, published in 1776, explained to the people living in the American

Colonies what was happening as a result of British rule in plain and common sense terms. He pointed out how British rule was obstructing the colonists from achieving the goals that they had of building a better life for themselves and future generations.

As a result of the wide-spread circulation of Paine's book, *Common Sense*, the majority of the people living in the American Colonies became aware of and understood the constraints British rule was having on their lives, and how it was affecting their ability to have the life that they were seeking when they came to America.

Thomas Paine was able to see and analyze, from a higher, broader vantage point, and in a systemic way, what was happening in America as Britain tightened her grip on their rule of the American Colonies. Paine was also able to express his views very clearly and concisely so that everyone could understand. Armed with this understanding, the Colonists could then make an informed decision on what needed to be done. Thus the beginning of America as a free democratic society; the foundation of our progress and success.

From this better understanding of the impact that British rule was having on their lives, the vast majority of Colonists rallied in support of the American Revolution.

Sacrificing and winning the American Revolution gave all Colonists the freedom and independence that they felt was needed to pursue a fulfilling life in America.

As these United States of America established its economy, educational system, and government, the country evolved from a collection of independent colonies into a nation that was to have a larger presence in the world community.

Throughout much of my lifetime, flourishing America offered increasing opportunities to its citizens, and the changes that were occurring provided the means for a continuing higher standard of living.

With progress often comes some effects or consequences, intended or otherwise, which may not be beneficial to us as citizens or to America as a whole. Remember the old adage, 'There is no free lunch'.

Some of America's progress has occurred with negative consequences.

Purpose
One of my major concerns is that 'now' may be the first time that the current generation of Americans will have a lower standard of living and a less fulfilling life than in prior generations.

In this book I will lay out some of the trends and conditions that exist that lead me to this concern. We Americans have built the greatest and most prosperous free society in the world, and want it to continue for many generations. There are some current issues that need to be fully understood and addressed to help assure the continuation of our progress for the benefit of all.

Here I attempt to provide a view of our current lives in America from a vantage point of 30,000 feet, where we can see more clearly the interrelationships between our government, business, globalization, our educational system, our work, our life-styles, and our values. All of

7

these systems are interrelated, and a change in one affects the others. Viewing this big picture of life in America, we can then make choices that are best for ourselves, and yet consider the impact on the rest of society.

This book attempts to paint a 'big picture view' of America as it is today, as Thomas Paine did when he outlined the threats and challenges for the American Colonists to achieving their life's objectives. Our challenge as Americans is similar today. We need to gain a better understanding of what is happening in our world, how it affects us, and how to best deal with it to achieve our life's goals.

Changes to America have snuck up on us, occurring slowly over time.

Gradual Change
The well-known 'frog' analogy describes gradual change and its long-term effects. If you put a frog in a pot of water, place it on the stove, and apply increasing heat gradually over a long period of time, the frog will eventually die without knowing what was happening in the process, and often without much pain and suffering. The frog gradually adapts to the hotter environment, until the breaking point is reached, it can no longer adapt, and it dies.

Many of us experience changes in a similar way, without complete awareness, and often little initial pain. We tend to adjust to changes as they occur, and go on with life, often without thinking. We just react, accept, and go with the flow. The cumulative effect of gradual changes are often what causes long-term problems.

A Perspective

In this book, I attempt to bring a higher and broader view of America. I will highlight from 30,000 feet, some of the trends and current conditions under which we are now living. I will also provide some insights into how we can better understand and thereby better navigate the current world to achieve our goals.

We will look at our current government, economy, global environment, business and work environments, and educational systems, as well as our current life style and values, to see how each now affects our lives, how they are interrelated, and what we might want to change to give us the kind of life that we want for ourselves and future generations.

We can begin to work to change as individuals the things that we can personally control that might be detrimental to us and to future generations. Then we can consider what we might need to work together to change for the future that we do not have direct control or individual influence over.

More and more complete information builds awareness and better decision making. That is the ultimate purpose of this book.

We begin by looking at how our government has changed since its inception, and how some of these changes might affect our ability to achieve our life's goals today.

Chapter 2
Our Government

Together and with a common purpose, generations of Americans have worked to build the greatest country in the world on a strong foundation of an inclusive and participatory democracy. As a result, America has enjoyed unprecedented growth and prosperity, economically, politically, and socially.

American citizens have benefited by enjoying one of the highest standards of living in the world, and one of the freest societies.

In order to assure that America's progress continues, it is important to understand the foundation of America's success, and identify any current issues that might endanger our continuing as the 'land of opportunity', personal freedom, and self-determination.

The Purpose of our Government
Our nation's Founding Fathers set forth the basic principles for the establishment of a democracy in America. These principles are contained in the U.S. Constitution and the Bill of Rights. These documents have served as America's governing principles since the Revolution and the subsequent founding of the United States of America.

The U.S. Constitution, was signed on September 17, 1787 by the Founding Fathers, and subsequently ratified by all the original 13 Colonies by 1789.

The Constitution established the governing principles of the United States of America, and established the supreme law of the land. The U.S. Constitution laid out the principles for the separation of powers within the government's three branches.

Branch	Authority
Legislative	Makes Laws, originates spending bills, impeaches officials, and approves treaties
Executive	Provides national defense and foreign policy, enforces federal laws, and makes governmental appointments
Judicial	Interprets the Constitution, reviews laws, decides cases involving state's rights, assures laws are upheld and justice prevails, and assures due process under the law for all citizens

The Constitution clearly defined the role of the Federal Government and the role of State Governments.

The Federal Government was to provide services only in areas that the states could not, such as national defense, the overall protection of individual rights, and other limited services. The primary right of supremacy for each state to govern was to be protected under the U.S. Constitution.

The Constitution has been amended twenty-seven times since its original ratification to deal with specific issues. The Bill of Rights (amendments 1-10) was added to define the basic individual freedoms of Americans. Other amendments were added to address national issues such as abolishing slavery, giving women the right to vote, and giving youth at the age of eighteen the right to vote.

The Constitution and its amendments have served to provide a framework for how the American people were to be governed in our democracy. Basic freedoms, sovereignty, and self-determination for both the country and for each citizen, are the overriding principles that undergird our American Democracy.

Democracy in America
As Alexis de Tocqueville so accurately summarized in his book *Democracy in America*, democracy is not free and is very dependent on:
1. its citizens continuing to be very actively involved in local governments, and
2. their willingness to make decisions that are for the common good above individual self-interests.

Tocqueville referred to this principle as 'enlightened self-interest'. Without it, he felt that a democracy would not survive.

Tocqueville recognized that democracy in America was an 'experiment' in governing since, at no other time in history, had any nation had such a degree of freedom and self-determination that America offered.

Letting the states govern its citizens in all matters that affect its residents, and keeping the role of the Federal Government in check were fundamental underlying principles of our American Democracy.

So where do we stand today in the status and evolution of our democratic government?

The Federal Government
Some of the characteristics of our current Federal Government are:

- **It is large-**the annual federal budget is in excess of $3.9 trillion and represents 21% of the total U.S. economy. The Federal Government is also the U.S.'s largest employer with over 2.7 million employees.
- **It is involved in many aspects of our lives-**an ever-increasing number of laws about many more aspects of our lives continue to be enacted by the federal government.
- **All citizen are not equally represented-**business and special interests have a disproportionate amount of influence on government legislation.
- **There is increasing polarization-**both within the legislative branch (the Congress and Senate), and between the legislative and executive branches, that prevents critical national issues from being addressed effectively.
- **Money and political power are primary influences on government policy-**lobbyists reign supreme in Washington, and are a major influence on most major federal priorities and legislation.
- **National interests have been supplanted by special interests-**vote getting and pork barrel legislation continue to be practiced extensively in the legislative process, rather than legislation for the common good.

- **The U.S. national debt exceeds $17.6 trillion-** compared to the annual GDP of $16.7 trillion, or 105% of GDP. It is projected to increase to $22.4 trillion by 2020.
- **National political campaigns now cost hundreds of millions of dollars and are approaching billions-** state and local campaigns are setting records as well, preventing most Americans from holding public office, and creating a governing system where outcomes are determined by money. The 2016 presidential campaign expenditures will very likely exceed one billion dollars.
- **About 50% of Americans receive some government benefit-**increasing our dependence on government, reducing personal initiative and self-sufficiency. This also further increases the size of the federal government.
- **The Federal Government is watching us-**from the revelations of Eric Snowden and others, it has come to light that various branches of the Federal Government are routinely looking at the activities of many Americans through telephone and internet records. This is done without their knowledge or approval from the judicial system. It is done in the name of the 'war on terror'. It has also been recently revealed that the U.S. has been spying on other countries including a number of allies. Our personal freedoms are at increasingly at risk.

What do these current conditions within of our government mean for our democracy and for us a

14

American citizens? Who are the winners and who are the losers? Let's look at some of these issues in more detail to determine what they mean to us, and how they affect our lives.

Government Size

As outlined in the U.S. Constitution, the role the Federal Government was to play in governing America was to provide only those services that the states could not. These services were to include national defense, treaties and trade agreements with other nations, a federal judicial system to assure that the Constitution was upheld and that every American receives a fair trial, and other administrative functions to assure a smooth running government.

When we look at the size of a government, it can be measured in a number of ways. Its size can be measured relative to its role in governing, the size of its population, or to its economic output. In economic terms, the size of government is often measured in terms of annual government expenditures relative to its GDP or Gross Domestic Product. A nation's GDP represents the sum total of all goods and services produced by that nation in one year (referred to as annual GDP).

Both in absolute dollar terms and as a percent of GDP, the amount of federal spending has grown significantly over the past several generations. Beginning in the late 1930's and early 1940's federal spending grew as a result of the New Deal programs of President Franklin Roosevelt in response to the Great Depression.

Federal spending took a second major step up beginning in the late1960's with the advent of the 'Great Society' under the Johnson administration. During this period many new social programs were started and some existing ones were expanded. New programs initiated during this period included Medicare, Medicaid, disability benefits, a Head-Start program for preschoolers, and federal support for higher education. At the time many of these programs were aimed at reducing poverty in America.

The late 1960's and early 1970's was a period when America was financing both the 'Great Society' and the Vietnam War, causing Federal Government expenditures to increase significantly. However, expenditures did not go down after the war as they had in prior periods.

The annual federal budget now represents from 20-24% of GDP. Prior to the 1940's it had averaged about 4% of GDP, and prior to the mid-1960's about 10%.

Federal Government spending now appears to have made a permanent change to this higher level. Annual Federal Government expenditures have now averaged between 20% and 24% of GDP for about the past 50 years. The chart below shows the progressive increases in Federal Government spending over time.

Chart S.04f: Federal Spending since the Founding

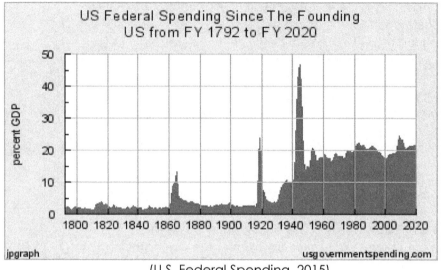

(U.S. Federal Spending, 2015)

The major Federal Government expenditures, based on current budget projections are:

Budget Item	Percent of Budget
Health care	27%
Pensions & Social Security	25%
Defense	22%
Welfare Payments	10%
Interest on Deficit	6%
Education	4%

From 2000 to 2010, Federal Government spending grew from $21,875 per person to $30,543 per person, or an increase of 44%.

During this same ten year period, wages of middle class Americans were essentially flat. Federal spending is projected to increase further to $35,604 per person by 2020.

The Winners of a larger Federal Government
Those who benefit from a large Federal Government include: government employees; those who receive direct federal benefits such as health care, disability payments, income assistance payments such as earned income tax credits and child tax credits; students who receive education credits and Pell Grants; children of low income families who receive Medicaid health insurance; and retirees who receive Medicare health insurance and Social Security income.

All Americans benefit from a strong U.S. defense, especially with the current terrorism activities around the world.

All Americans also benefit from a strong and modern national infrastructure including roads, bridges, and rail transportation. Americans benefit from government supported research and development (R&D), as that is where space exploration, the global positioning system (GPS), and the internet were developed. Many other innovations that we accept as common place today were the result of government supported R&D.

 In recent decades, the Federal Government has fallen short in investing sufficiently in both infrastructure and R&D. As a result of lower government funding of both, the U.S. has fallen behind other countries. This puts the U.S. at a competitive disadvantage in the global economy.

Most of the interstate highway system in the U.S., was built the 1960's. Today much of our highway and other major infrastructure is in need of major repair and upgrading.

Only a very small portion of the federal budget is now spent on maintaining and improving our infrastructure as it continues to age. China and Japan are now world leaders in high-speed rail, as the U.S. struggles to develop its first major system. Without modern and well maintained infrastructure, the U.S. will be at a competitive disadvantage with other countries.

Fewer Resources Available
As a higher percent of our nation's GDP is spent on government, less is available for other purposes such as investments, research and development, and additional income for individuals to improve their standard of living.

As the size of our Federal Government continues to grow, more of the government's expenditures will likely have to be financed with debt, as incomes and tax revenues are not growing as fast as the budget of the federal government.

Our economy has not been able to support its level of government spending without borrowing for quite some time, even before the 2008 recession.

Increasing taxes on U.S. citizens will only make more of them dependent on government services. This will result in further increases in government spending, and higher deficits.

Taxing the wealthy more is unlikely to happen with the political influence that businesses and the wealthy currently have on the government. A higher tax alone on the wealthy will not solve the problem of growing government expenditures. In 2014, the top 20% of all wage earners in the U.S. paid 84% of the total amount of income taxes collected. 49% of current income tax filers pay no income taxes at all. (Saunders, 2015)

Government Debt
With Federal Government spending remaining high, and government borrowing continuing to increase, the amount of interest paid on the federal debt will continue to increase. This drains money away from other needs. Over 40% of government spending today is with borrowed money.

According to recent data:

Forty-three (43) cents of every dollar spent by the Federal Government is borrowed. This amount is about 4 times the rate it was in 1980. Between 2007 and 2011, the rate of federal borrowing increased from thirty (30) cents to thirty-eight (38) cents per dollar spent. At this pace, the historical trend of deficit spending continues at a disturbing rate. (Rugy, 2011)

The Federal Government has had a budget deficit every year from 1980 to1997. The surplus that finally emerged in 1998 was produced by increased tax revenues from a sustained economic expansion, not from a tax increase. By 2001 the Federal Government was again operating with a deficit and has been every year since.

With record low interest rates since the economic crisis of 2008, the interest on the federal debt has not had a significant effect on the overall federal budget. As

20

interest rates return to historical levels, federal interest payments will become an increasing burden on the federal government's finances, further restricting funds for other uses.

Many countries such as Greece, Spain, Panama, Japan, Italy and Brazil, are experiencing various degrees of financial distress due to high levels of government debt.

Even Puerto Rico, a commonwealth of the United States is in danger of financial collapse due to high government debt. The U.S. is not immune from financial distress, as we learned from the 2008 Global Financial Crisis. There is significant risk of additional financial distress if we continue to spend beyond our ability to pay.

A collapse of any government, no matter how small or seemingly insignificant, could destroy confidence in the world's financial systems and lead to a panic and another global financial crisis. With our global economic connectedness and interdependency, what happens in one part of the world has effects on many others.

Since the end of the Second World War, the U.S. has been seen as a safe haven, both economically and politically. As we continue to accumulate more Federal Government debt, we also put our country in danger, as there are limits to everything. Continuing to increase government debt in the U.S. is not in the long-term best interests of America or Americans. Every situation has a 'tipping point'.

No person or nation can continue to live beyond their means for an extended period of time and not suffer some consequences.

Dependence on Government

One of the major reasons for increased Federal Government expenditures is the growth of entitlement programs that began with the New Deal, and grew with the Great Society under President Johnson. These programs were initiated to provide a financial 'safety net' for Americans during the Depression in the 1930's, and to lift Americans out of poverty in the 1960's. Most have continued, and have expanded over time.

In 1960, expenditures for federal anti-poverty programs (more commonly known as welfare) represented 0.4% of GDP. In 1980 they were 1.9% of GDP, and in 2010, 4.4% of GDP.

Today more Americans receive various forms of government assistance. There are a number of reasons for this, some are economic, while others are social.

Some of the Federal Government benefits such as Social Security and Medicare, are benefits that American workers paid for during their working years, and now collect during retirement. Other government benefits are merely ways to redistribute wealth, and/or to make up for income inequality. These types of benefits include refundable tax credits such as Earned Income Tax credits, Additional Child Tax Credits, and Education Credits.

The growing financial dependency of Americans on government support will likely not change for several generations, as the U.S. population continues to age, income inequality grows, and job opportunities and incomes for the middle class continue to decline.

In 1950, 28.5% of Americans received some meaningful financial support from the government; in 1970 it was 52.4%; in 2007 it was 58.2%; and today it is 67.3%. More Americans are becoming more dependent on government for more of their basic needs. (Shilling, 2015)

With increased dependency on government, America runs the risk of becoming a 'nanny state' where Americans become dependent on the government from cradle-to-grave, rather than being self-reliant. Our strong values of self-reliance and independence were the foundation that built a strong and prosperous America. This growing dependence on government by more Americans threatens are future economic security as a nation as well.

A growing Federal Government tends to feed upon itself. As we spend more on government, and thereby take more resources away from businesses and individuals, we limit the individual's ability to provide for themselves, and risk destroying the spirit of self-sufficiency, innovation, and risk taking.

Entitlement
An unintended consequence of greater dependency on the Federal Government by more and more Americans is the evolution of an 'entitlement mentality'.

The size and reach of our Federal Government has conditioned some Americans to expect more from the government. A number of Americans now expect federal and state governments to provide them with many of their basic needs such as food, work, health care, education, housing, and transportation.

There is a risk that the spread of this 'entitlement mentality' could destroy individual drive and the sense of personal responsibility, thus weakening the foundations of our American society. These personal characteristics are even more important today, as the U.S. must compete in a global economy. America needs its entire citizenship actively engaged in continuing to build a better America now and for future generations.

The bottom line is that there are inherent dangers in a large and growing government. We need to be aware and guard against these dangers. We need to balance the essential role that the Federal Government should play, with what we as citizens should accept as our personal responsibility. These are the principles that America was founded on, and that is what our Constitution defines as the role of the Federal Government.

Since the 1960's we appear to have gotten out of balance with respect to our dependence upon the government for many of the things that we had provided for ourselves and our families in past generations.

Government Regulation
Our lives have become more complex in the last several decades due to the advancement of technology and associated social changes. Americans have experienced a significant increase in the number of and complexity of laws and regulations about more and more aspects of their lives.

24

Some of the increase in the number of laws and regulations has been in response to new technology. Much of the increase, however, represents a further encroachment by the Federal Government into more aspects of our lives.

Laws have also become more complex as well as more specific, restrictive, and more detailed. This legal trend has reduced the amount of judgment that can be applied to account for specific conditions or circumstances. A number and scope of federal laws enacted in the past several decades has begun to encroach on state's rights as well.

This major increase in the number, nature, and complexity of federal regulations has increased both the cost of regulating compliance and the cost of litigation. These costs have further added to the cost of federal and state governments.

Over the ten year period from 2000 to 2011, the Federal Government issued just under 38,000 new rules. To publish the Code of Federal Regulations at the end of 2011 it took 169,301 pages, compared to 71,244 pages in 1975. An increase of 169% in the number of pages of federal regulations. It was estimated that it costs $1.236 trillion to comply with these regulations or the equivalent of $15,586 for each household in the U.S. in 2008.

During the first three years of the Obama administration, 2009-2011, The Federal Code of Regulations increased by 11,327 pages or by 7.4% over the prior period. (Starr, 2012)

It has been said that laws and lawyers make law breakers. The U.S. has the largest number of lawyers per capita than any other country in the world, with 281 lawyers per 100,000 population compared with Britain with 94, France with 33, and Japan with 7.

In the 113th U.S. Congress, 41% of its members are lawyers. This high concentration of lawyers contributes to an over emphasis on writing laws which have become increasingly more complex, specific, and restrictive. This approach to legislation limits American's ability to apply practical common sense to many of life's real situations, limits personal freedoms, and increases the cost of enforcement.

Americans in Prison
The U.S. also has the highest number of its citizens incarcerated per capita than any other country in the world, including oppressive regimes. The U.S. has less than 5% of the world's population but has about 25% of the world's prisoners.

There are currently about 2.3 million persons in U.S. federal and state prisons, and another 4.8 million people on probation. This represents almost 3% of the total U.S. adult population.

Of the total number of U.S. prisoners, about 460,000 or 20% are considered dangerous and were imprisoned for violent crimes. The majority of the prisoners do not pose a threat to society. With rehabilitation, many of them could become positive contributors to society, rather than a financial burden.

The annual cost to keep each prisoner is about $68.000 per year. In addition, some of these prisoners have families who are collecting government benefits since the spouse is not available to provide support. The U.S.

economy loses between $57 billion and $65 billion of output each year as a result of excess incarceration. (Palazzolo, 2015)

High rates of incarceration in the U.S. have been cited as one of the contributing factors in the breakdown of working-class families, especially among African American families.

Causes of the high incarceration rate in the U.S. range from lack of employment opportunities for the disadvantaged, increases in 'white collar' crime, the tendency to impose long sentences, and minimum sentencing guidelines. An ineffective rehab program, as well as an ineffective legal and judicial system also contribute to the high rate of incarceration.

Since 1980, the U.S. prison population has grown four-fold. Some of the public policy changes that have had an impact on this increase include:

- enactment of 'tough on crime laws',
- increased length of sentences,
- mandatory minimum sentencing,
- the 'war on drugs',
- the 'three-strike' law,
- reductions in early release programs,
- decreases in budgets for rehabilitation.

Legalizing some minor drugs, more effective rehab programs for offenders, shorter sentences for non-violent crimes, and more realistic sentencing guidelines, would be areas to consider changing in order to reduce the social and the financial burdens of incarceration. Americans should not be burdened with the cost of a high rate of incarceration when many of these prisoners could become contributing members of society. Two-thirds of the female prisoners are single parents, which causes other long-lasting social problems. (The Economist , 2015)

In a recent book, *Dreamland: The True Tail of America's Opiate Epidemic,* the author concludes, based on extensive research, that when drug dependency occurs from either legal or illegal drugs, it needs to be dealt with by the medical profession rather than with the criminal system. Dependency on legal drugs often leads to the use of illegal drugs, and support of the criminal element. The author further concludes that the odds are much higher in favor of rehabilitation over incarceration to effectively address the drug problem in the U.S. Over the past decade, incarceration has not worked, and has had quite severe consequences both for families, society in general, and for government expenditures. (Quinones, 2015)

Business Regulation
The United States is still one of the best countries in which to do business. However, in the past several decades, the U.S. business regulatory system has become more complex. There are often overlapping government regulatory agencies, which make it difficult and increasingly more expensive to do business in the U.S.

Recent Federal regulations such as the Dodd-Frank bill and the Patient Protection and Affordable Care Act, are so complex, restrictive, and comprehensive, that they add administrative costs to businesses, and additional enforcement and monitoring costs to the government. The legislation in both cases was needed, but resulted being much more complex than can be cost-effectively managed by businesses or by the government. When drafting legislation, consideration must be given to the benefits as well as the costs, including administrative and enforcement costs.

A number of governmental agencies such as the EPA (Environmental Protection Agency, (EEOC) Equal Employment Opportunity Commission, CPSC (Consumer Product Safety Commission), (FTC) Federal Trade Commission, FDA (Food and Drug Administration), NLRB (National Labor Relations Board), OSHA (Occupational Safety and Health Administration), and the ICC (Interstate Commerce Commission) are some of the federal agencies that are making it more difficult and more expensive to do business in the U.S.

The U.S. has one of the highest rates of corporate income taxes in the world. This has driven some U.S. companies to merge with foreign companies and establish corporate headquarters in that country. The merged company can thereby avoid paying the high rate of U.S. corporate taxes. This process is referred to as 'inversion'. Current tax laws also make it costly for U.S. corporations to bring profits earned in foreign countries back to the U.S., so many keep the profits in the foreign country and therefore do not invest in the U.S. but rather in foreign countries.

Many laws that affect U.S. businesses have become so complex that it takes a staff of lawyers to understand them and assure that all the requirements are met. The Dodd-Frank law, passed as a result of the 2008 Global Financial Crisis, is 2,700 pages long. Many corporate lawyers are needed to interpret it so that companies can meet the requirements.

The Patient Protection and Affordable Care Act (aka Obama Care) is 906 pages long and most legislators who approved had not read it.

With growing complexity and more laws that regulate more and more of both our business and our personal lives, we live more now under the 'rule of lawyers' rather than the rule of law. (Shilling, 2015)

Government and Business
Over the past several decades the ties between government and business have strengthened. These stronger ties have given businesses influence over government policy and legislation. A somewhat codependent relationship now exists between government and business. This relationship is often detrimental to the interests of many Americans, and to the general common-good of the United States. Lobbying to influence legislation and promote special interests has been a major mechanism used by business to influence Washington.

Political lobbying is defined as the use of paid professional advocates by organizations to argue for specific legislation before decision making bodies and their representatives, such as the United States Congress.

Washington lobbyists represent primarily corporations and other special interest groups. Many of today's lobbyists are highly paid lawyers and former legislators who have personal relationships with members of Congress.

Since the 1970's lobbying in Washington has grown rapidly. In 2014 there were 12,281 registered lobbyists, bringing in an estimated $9 billion annually.

Almost $30 billion was spent on lobbying from 1998 to 2010. Major industries and expenditures were:

Industry	Billion $U.S.	% of total
Fin., Ins. & Real Estate	4.27	15%
Health Care	4.22	15%
Misc. Business	4.15	14%
Comm./Electronics	3.50	12%
Transportation	2.25	8%

A number of large U.S. law firms, paid by corporations and special interest groups, are involved in many aspects of lobbying, including providing assistance in writing legislation that favors their clients.

According to the website, Opensecrets.org, the following organizations and corporations were the major spenders on lobbying in 2014:

Organization	Millions $U.S.
US Chamber of Commerce	$124.1
National Association of Realtors	$55.1
Blue Cross Blue Shield	$21.9
American Hospital Assoc.	$20.8
American Medical Assoc.	$19.7
National Assoc. of Broadcasters	$18.4
Nat'l. Cable and Telecommunications	$17.5

Organization	Millions $U.S.
Comcast	$17.0
Google	$16.8
Boeing	$16.8
Pharmaceutical Mfgs. of America	$16.6
United Technologies	$15.7
General Electric	$15.2
Business Roundtable	$14.8
CVS Health	$14.8

(OpenSecrets.org, 2015)

It is difficult to imagine how the average American has a chance to be represented in Congress against this kind of political influence.

Attempts at legislation to limit and control lobbying, have only led lobbyists to develop more sophisticated strategies. It is estimated that the actual number of lobbyists is around 100,000, when the 'underground' lobbyists are included. (WikipediA, 2015)

Health Care Lobbying
A recent example of the influence lobbying has on Federal legislation, is the Patient Affordable Health Care Act (aka Obama Care).

Steven Brill in his recent book, *America's Bitter Pill*, describes in detail how the pharmaceutical companies, health care insurance companies, medical professionals, and manufacturers of medical supplies and equipment all worked to shape the Patient Protection and Affordable Care Act for their benefit. As seen from the two previous charts, the health care industry has been and continues to be a major supporter of lobbyists.

Brill details in *America's Bitter Pill,* the size and scope of the health care industry in the U.S. Annual revenues of the industry are over $3 trillion. The health care industry employs one sixth of the U.S. workforce, and represents the largest single expenditure for the average American family. (Brill, America's Bitter Pill, 2015)

 The stakes are therefore high for the industry, and they have been willing to spend billions to try to insure that their interests are well represented in any legislation that affects them. The health care industry is now the largest spending lobbyist group in Washington, surpassing the financial industry.

The total annual expenditures for health care in the U.S. are more than the expenditures of Japan, Germany, France, the U.K., Italy, Canada, Brazil, Spain, and Australia **combined.**

One consequence of high health care costs for Americans, is that 60% of the one million personal bankruptcies each year are a result of unpaid health care expenses.

Since the year 2000, health care premiums have increased four times faster than wages. The increase in costs has not generally resulted in improved health or health care for Americans. The U.S. ranks 31st in life expectancy and 28th in infant mortality in the world. Even though America spends the most on health care per capita, and in total dollars than any other country in the world, the benefits are not the best.

The influence that the health care industry has on the federal legislative process is a contributing factor to the high costs of health care in the U.S.

Today the average family health care insurance policy costs **$11,841 per year. This is more than a minimum wage job pays in a year.**

Another example of how the Federal Government and the health care industry have worked together to keep the cost of health care higher for the consumer and profits higher for the providers is a **law that currently prohibits Medicare from negotiating prices with the drug companies.** This restriction was part of the Medicare part D legislation that was passed in 2006. Americans pay more for the same drugs, manufactured by the same companies, than do citizens of Canada, Mexico, and many other countries.

Much of the Patient Protection and Affordable Care Act was written by the health care industry to protect their interests and insure higher profits. Many deals were made in the legislative process which make health care more expensive for the consumer and more profitable for the providers.

The Privileged Club
Some of the above facts suggest that the Federal Government has become less effective in governing, less representative of the American people, more influenced by money and power, and limited in terms of who can practically participate.

Issues such as: ideological polarization, lobbying, the lack of voice and accessibility for many Americans, the influence of money, the cost of political campaigns, pork barrel legislation, uncontrolled spending, high deficits, the lack of realistic budgets, and the failure to address critical national issues such as infrastructure and immigration reform, are all signs of both ineffectiveness and the lack of equal access to the political process for all Americans.

Critical national issues such as deficits, illegal immigration, infrastructure rebuilding, income tax reform, budgeting, and educational reform are not now effectively being addressed by our federal government. This is due to a large degree to an increasing unwillingness of members of Congress to work together, regardless of their party affiliation, for the common good of America. This is the job that they were elected to do, and they are failing.

These current conditions in Washington are affecting both the present and the future of Americans. We as a nation are moving further away from a true representative democracy, and setting the stage for further separation between the rulers (big money interest groups and the elite class of legislators) and the people they are changed with governing.

The Bottom Line
Today when we look at our Federal Government from 30,000 feet, we see that it is much larger in terms of expenditures, employees, and deeper in its reach into the lives of Americans than several generations ago.

Our government has become less democratic and less representative of all citizens, as business and special interests groups have gained a disproportionate influence.

Our Federal Government is more intrusive in our daily lives with the ability, without our knowledge or legal authority, to track our every movement through the use of telecommunications technology and other means.

Our legislative and judicial systems have focused on more restrictive laws and penalties for individual crimes, causing our prison populations to grow four-fold over several decades, preventing even minor offenders and their families from having a productive life, thus putting undue burdens on society.

In the last two decades there has been a significant increase in the number and complexity of federal laws and regulations affecting both individuals and businesses. This has made it more difficult and more costly to do business in America, and has further limited an individual's ability to apply common sense when it comes to various choices.

Participation in government by holding public office is much less possible today for the average American. Those who can be public servants is limited by the high cost of campaigning, and is fueled by millions of dollars of special interest money available to those in power.

Every day the Federal Government borrows money to cover its day-to-day expenses. Currently over forty cents of each dollar of Federal Government spending is borrowed. This increases the federal budget deficit each and every day. The growing deficit reduces the flexibility of the government, puts additional financial burden on the next generations, and adds financial risk to the U.S. economy.

The Federal Government has become more polarized and dysfunctional, preventing critical national issues from being adequately addressed.

More Americans are becoming increasingly more dependent on the federal government. This trend, if left unchecked, will further destroy personal initiative and foster an entitlement society. This growing dependency will in turn further increase government expenditures and deficits.

When we compare the status of our Federal Government today with the principles our Founding Fathers established when they formed this democracy, we appear to be on a divergent path away from sound democratic principles.

The status of our Federal Government today has a significant impact on the ability of many Americans to achieve 'the American Dream'. These current issues that have been pointed out need to be considered when we look at what we want to accomplish in our life in America, and how **our government** can either help or hinder us.

A recent poll taken by the *Wall Street Journal* and CBS, indicates that 65% of the Americans polled feel that the Federal Government is taking the U.S. in the wrong direction, and only 28% felt that the government was going in the right direction. This suggests that most Americans know current reality. (Hook, 2015)

Let's turn now to our global environment and how it impacts our lives.

Chapter 3
Our Global Environment

Globalization is defined as the interdependence of countries and regions of the world in areas of economic commerce. In the past several decades we have become a truly global economy, where what happens economically in most counties has an impact on many other countries and the world as a whole.

Growth of Globalization
Some economists attribute the rapid growth of global economic activity since World War II to the removal of protectionist measures that had constricted world trade since 1913. Others cite a number of enablers of globalization, such as improvements in transportation and communications, and the wide-spread use of technologies such as the internet. (Krugman, 1995)

Since 1950, there has been a rapid acceleration in the growth of world trade. The chart below shows the explosion of international trade since the 1950's.

Year	Total World Exports- billions of $U.S.	Cumulative Increase
1950	$ 61.8	-
1960	$ 130.9	111.8%
1970	$ 318.0	414.6%
1980	$ 2,049.4	3,216.2%
1990	$ 3,495.7	5,564.7%
2000	$ 6,452.6	10,341.1%
2010	$ 15,300.7	24,568.4%
2013	$ 18,817.7	30,349.4%

(Stastica, 2015)

Since 1950 the world's population has grown from 2.55 billion people to 7.3 billion, or by 186 %. During the same period, world trade has increased over 300 fold.

Global trade now represents 24.2% of total global GDP. GDP or Gross National Product is defined as the total annual value of goods and services produced by a country as measured in dollars.

Today about a quarter of the world's total production is traded each year, compared to only 1.1% in 1960. Over this 55 year period, global trade has become a major part of the economies of most countries. As a result of this growth, global trade now influences many country's economic and political decisions. (Worldometers, 2015)

Free Trade Agreements have been the vehicle that have provided the regulatory and legal framework to make global trade on today's scale possible.

Free Trade Agreements
Since the end of WW II, there has been a growing world-wide-interest in increasing the amount of economic activity between countries and amongst geographical regions. The reasons varied depending on the maturity of the economy.

Developed economies such as the U.S. and Europe were seeking new markets and new sources of lower cost materials.

Developing countries such as China and India were seeking ways to improve their economies, attract foreign investment, and thereby improve the standard of living for their citizens.

A common belief held by both developed and developing countries was that all countries who participated in global trade could benefit. Many countries were therefore very open to negotiating what were seen as mutually beneficial trade agreements.

The movement towards more trade between nations started in earnest in 1947 with international trade discussions between the U.S. and other developed countries. Preliminary trade agreements were reached under the umbrella of GATT (General Agreement on Tariffs and Trade). These agreements focused primarily on the issues of negotiating: tariffs, how business was to be conducted between countries, and how disputes were to be settled.

Over the course of the next several decades, discussions, negotiations, and agreements continued. As benefits were experienced by those countries who participated in free trade, other countries joined in the process.

Over time, trade agreements and negotiations evolved into the formation of the World Trade Organization (WTO) in 1994. It was established as a formal organization to provide a forum for world trade negotiations, as well as a body to investigate and resolve trade disputes between countries. There are now 163 permanent member nations of the World Trade Organization.

Trade agreements have also been negotiated with groups of countries in geographical regions such as, NAFTA-1994 (North American Free Trade Agreement), and CAFTA-2004 (U.S.-Central American Free Trade Agreement). The establishment of the European Union (EU) in 2003 and the introduction of the Euro currency in1999 were the result of the European nations' desire to form an integrated free-trade network throughout Europe. All of these trade agreements have been focused on improving the free-flow of goods and services between countries by reducing tariffs and other trade barriers such as quotas and restraints.

Global trade has a major influence not only on an individual country's economy, but also, increasingly, on the world economy. The growth of global trade has made some nations economically dependent on others, and has created a more globally interdependent world.

The economy of China is an example of global interdependency resulting from economic globalization. The Chinese economy today is very dependent on the economies of the countries and regions to which it exports products, such as the U.S., Europe, and other Asian countries.

The Chinese economy is primarily production and export oriented, and depends on other countries for many of the raw materials it uses to produce its goods.

China is the world's largest consumer of copper, and a major importer of oil, wood, electronic equipment, and machinery. China is the world's largest producer of steel. It needs world sources of supply for copper, oil, coal, and other materials.

China needs world markets for exporting steel, as it produces much more steel than it consumes. China needs world export markets for a broad range of other products such as clothing and electronics, which it also produce in excess of what it consumes.

Exports represent over 30% of China's economy, and consumption only 36%. In the U.S., consumption represents 72% of its total economic activity. If China did not have a large export market for its products, the Chinese economy would be much smaller, and fewer Chinese would be working.

Effects of Free Trade
Free-trade agreements have generally lowered import duties and eliminated other trade barriers between countries. These agreements have given Americans access to a greater variety of goods and services and at generally lower costs.

When I first learned to drive a car as a teenager, there was the choice of three major brands of automobiles in the U.S. You could buy General Motors, Chrysler, or Ford. Today, as a result of free trade and economic globalization, there are the additional choices of Volkswagen, Toyota, Hyundai, Honda, Kia, BMW, Mazda, Fiat, and Volvo, as well as luxury brands such as Mercedes, Porsche, Jaguar, Land Rover, and Maserati. Free trade has also given us better quality cars with more features, and at more competitive costs.

The availability of more choices and lower costs is also true for many other categories of goods and services. The American consumer now has more choices, comparable or better quality, and lower prices than prior to economic globalization. Global competition forces all companies to continue to improve in order to survive. Global competition has directly benefited the American consumer.

There are, however, some aspects of free trade and economic globalization that are not necessarily good for every American or for America overall.

Offshoring

As a by-product of free trade agreements and economic globalization, many U.S. companies now use off-shoring, or the purchasing of materials and services from foreign countries, to lower their costs. Offshoring is defined as the foreign sourcing for materials and components for products made in a home country. Autos assembled in the U.S., as an example, contain an average of 30% of their content which comes from countries outside of the U.S.

There are many other examples of products that are made in the U.S. but have a high content of foreign produced materials and components. Products made in the U.S. such as construction machinery, machine tools, engines, appliances, and computers use foreign produced components.

Offshoring is one of the consequences of free trade and economic globalization which has both positive and negative effects for the U.S. Effects are positive for the consumer, the corporate executive, and the shareholder, but there are some negative effects for both the U.S. worker, the U.S. economy, and the U.S. government.

Let's look at some of the effects that economic globalization has had on Americans and on the U.S. economy overall.

Negative Effects of Economic Globalization
The effects of expanding economic globalization that could be viewed as negative to the U.S. and to Americans include:

- **An Increase in Foreign Investment by U.S. Companies** and a decrease in investments in the U.S. This limits job growth in the U.S.
- **An Increase in Investments in the U.S. by Foreign Countries** gives foreign countries control of U.S. assets and workers.
- **A Negative U.S. Balance of Trade** transfers U.S. dollars to other countries, giving them more control over the U.S. financial system and the U.S. economy.
- **Foreign Countries Supply Americans** with many products that were previously made in the U.S, such as clothing, toys, furniture, appliances, autos, steel, and electronics. This results in the loss of good paying manufacturing and support jobs in the U.S.
- **Loss of Manufacturing Expertise in the U.S.** for a number of products such as televisions, shoes, clothing, phones, computers, machine tools, and other electronic products. These products are no longer made in the U.S., or are made in much smaller volumes. This makes the U.S. more

vulnerable economically because it reduces America's 'know how', and makes the U.S. more dependent on foreign countries for more of what American's consume.

- **A Shift in Economic Growth from the U.S.** to developing countries limits opportunity for many American workers and slows economic development and growth in the U.S.
- **A Growing Dependence by the U.S.** on foreign made goods, making the U.S. more vulnerable to influences of foreign nations and weakening the U.S. economy.
- **An Increase in Global Competition for Labor and Knowledge Workers** reduces the employment and career opportunities for many American workers.

There are, however, some positive effects of globalization for some Americans, for U.S. businesses, and for many developing countries.

Positive Effects of Globalization
Some of the positive effects of economic globalization include:

- **The Emergence and Growth of Some Industries** in the U.S. such as shipping, rail transportation, warehousing, distribution, exporting, outsourcing, and logistics, as more goods are exported and imported.
- **Opportunities for Global Careers** as globalization has opened up opportunities for Americans to work for U.S. multi-national companies in the U.S.as well as in foreign countries.

- **Reduction in World Poverty** as higher standards of living for citizens in many developing countries result from economic globalization. Many nations are achieving a level of economic self-sufficiency that is good for them and for the world, as the need for foreign aid will decline.
- **Lower Costs** with globalization. Consumers in the U.S. have gained access to a greater variety of product choices and often at lower costs.
- **U.S. businesses** benefit as they have world markets in which to sell their products and services, access to lower cost materials, and lower cost production around the world.

Let's look in a bit more detail at the impact of the effects of economic globalization on the United States and its citizens.

Foreign Investment
As the momentum of economic globalization increased, more U.S. corporations saw opportunities to make investments in foreign countries. By doing so, they could take advantage of lower costs for products sold in the U.S. as well as establish a presence in developing countries to sell their products.

This movement to offshore manufacturing has resulted in a significant shift in corporate investments from the U.S. to foreign countries. This shift in investments has resulted in the loss of good paying manufacturing jobs for millions of American workers. Also, many knowledge and professional jobs were lost when U.S. companies set up both manufacturing and R&D operations in foreign countries.

In 2012, U.S. companies invested $388 billion in foreign countries, while foreign companies invested $166 billion in the U.S. This represents a net investment outflow from the U.S. of $222 billion. Surprisingly 74% of that U.S. foreign investment was in developed countries such as the U.K., Germany, Canada, and France. 26% of the total U.S. foreign investment was in developing countries such as China, India, Mexico, and Vietnam. (Jackson, 2013)

Looking at the history of investments by U. S. companies in foreign countries compared to the amounts that foreign countries invested in the U.S. we find an accelerating rate of foreign investment over time:

Year	Cumulative U.S. Investments in Foreign Countries (billions $)	Cumulative Investments in U.S. by Foreign Countries (billions $)
1982	207.8	124.7
1990	430.5	394.9
1995	699.0	535.6
2000	1,316.2	1,256.9
2005	2,247.0	1,634.1
2010	3,741.9	2,280.0
2012	4,453.3	2,650.8

(Ibarra-Caton, 2013)

From 1982 to 2012 the total cumulative investment by the U.S. in foreign countries was $4.45 trillion, compared to $2.65 trillion invested by foreign countries in the U.S. This represents a net **negative investment balance of $1.80 trillion** over this period.

In the last decade the net outflow of investments from the U.S. has further accelerated. During the ten year period from 2002 through 2012 foreign investments in the U.S. grew from $917.5 billion to $1,152.2 billion or by 25%. During this same period, U.S. investments in foreign countries grew by $2,992.9 billion or by 175.5% (United States Census Bureau, 2013)

As U.S. companies increased their foreign investments, their corporate profits increased significantly, and are now 12.5% of GDP compared to 7.9% of GDP in 1980. (Dolan, 2013)

The overall impact of the increase in foreign investments by U.S. companies over the past several decades has been that:

- Corporate growth and profits are now higher in real terms and as a percentage of GDP. Corporations are not only increasing profits thru globalization but also getting a bigger piece of the total economic pie.
- The decline in corporate investments in the U.S. has decreased the potential opportunity for job growth in the U.S., and has left its manufacturing capability and capacity at increased risk of further decline.
- Due to the imbalance in foreign investments (more outflow from the U.S. than inflow from foreign countries), foreign countries now control a larger amount of U.S. currency reserves and U.S. assets, giving them more influence over the U.S. economy.

- U.S. companies now have access to the lowest costs anywhere in the world, and the best people resources anywhere in the world, giving them a potential competitive advantage on a global basis.

The winners in the transition from national economies to global economies are U.S. companies and their shareholders. The losers are many U.S. workers, as there is less relative investment in the U.S., which decreases job opportunities. U.S. companies often invest in the most modern technologies in foreign countries, further eroding the competitiveness of their U.S. operations.

U.S. companies benefit from economic globalization by lowering their costs and gaining access to world markets to increase revenues and profits. They also gain from tax advantages by retaining and investing profits in foreign countries, and thereby avoid paying U.S. corporate income taxes.

Balance of Trade
Another potentially harmful effect of economic globalization on the U.S. is the negative balance of trade that the U.S. now has with most all of its trading partners. Every year the U.S. currently imports more goods and services than it exports.

A look at the trends in imports and exports tells the story:

Year	U.S. Exports	U.S. Imports	Balance
1960	25,940	22,432	+3,508
1965	35,285	30,621	+4,664
1970	56,640	54,386	+2,254
1975	132,585	120,181	+12,404
1980	271,834	291,241	**-19,407**
1985	289,070	410,950	**-121,880**
1990	538,233	616,097	**-80,864**
1995	794,387	890,771	**-96,384**
2000	1,075,321	1,447,837	**-372,517**
2005	1,286,022	2,000,267	**-714,245**
2010	1,853,606	2,348,263	**-494,658**
2014	1,635,090	2,850,471	**-505,047**

(Division, 2015)

1975 was the last year the U.S. had a positive net balance of trade. As a result, foreign countries now hold $12.8 trillion in U.S. currency reserves. The largest holders are: China ($3.9 trillion), Japan ($1.2 trillion). Saudi Arabia ($0.7 trillion), Switzerland ($0.6 trillion), Taiwan ($0.4 trillion), and South Korea ($0.4 trillion).

Since 1975, the U.S. has been transferring its wealth to other countries at an increasing rate. This transfer of wealth could have a negative impact on the U.S. economy, as foreign countries can buy (with our money) assets in the U.S., as well as influence interest and currency exchange rates. This situation is not good for most Americans or for the U.S. economy overall. With a continuing negative balance of trade, we are transferring our wealth, and running the risk of giving control of our financial system and economy to foreign countries.

Lower Costs

Thanks to economic globalization and the internet, we can now buy most anything we want, made anywhere in the world, at very competitive prices. For Americans as consumers this is good, as our dollar goes a lot farther than if we were restricted to purchasing only goods produced in the U.S. but it may not be the best for America as a whole.

Today over 90% of the shoes that Americans purchase are made outside of the United States, as well as all television sets, all T-shirts, most toys, most computers, most smart phones, and most other electronic devices.

In 2014 the fastest growing imports to the U.S. were meats, cereals, dairy products, tobacco, vehicles and perfumes. This is an indication that we are increasing our dependence on foreign countries for more of our basic needs, and in many industries where the U.S. has been historically very strong. (World's Richest Countries, 2015)

As of 2014, the largest categories of imports to the U.S. from foreign countries were:

Commodity	Total Imports	% of Total Imports
Oil	$356.3 bn	14.8%
Machinery	$330.9 bn	13.7%
Electronics	$319.9 bn	13.3%
Vehicles	$265.4 bn	11.0%
Medical Equip.	$76.3 bn	3.2%
Pharmaceuticals	$73.2 bn	3.0%
Gems, precious metals	$65.7 bn	2.7%
Furniture	$55.8 bn	2.3%

(The U.S. Largest Imports, 2015)

With the exception of oil (of which we consume more that we were capable of producing in the U.S. until recently) and gems and precious metals (which are not found in abundance in the U.S.), several generations ago, the U.S. had been the world leader in both design and manufacturing capabilities in all the of these categories.

It can be argued that Americans receive the benefit of lower prices for the goods that are now imported, and thereby improve their standard of living. However, with the hollowing out of U.S. manufacturing capabilities, and the loss of these industry jobs over the past several generations, the U.S. has suffered the loss of much of its middle class.

The loss of many higher paying U.S. 'blue-collar' production jobs, and resultant lower incomes has put many Americans in the position of having to buy lower cost imported goods to maintain their standard of living, and in many cases just to survive. This has been one of the unintended consequences of economic globalization for America and for many Americans.

The losers from economic globalization are many U.S. citizens, especially those in the lower strata of skills and income.

With to continued growth of economic globalization, the U.S. also risks losing its position as a strong economy and economic power, as it continues to lose its capability to produce many products that are critical to a strong, broad-based economy.

America is rapidly becoming a nation of consumers only and not producers of what we consume. If we continue on this path, the U.S. will likely be unable to provide full employment opportunities for its population of workers now and in future generations.

The more imported goods Americans purchase, the less inclined U.S. companies will be to reinvestment in production technology and capacity in the U.S. **In the long run the U.S. risks losing a viable economy.**

Loss of Expertise
Over time, as we lose the expertise to manufacture, we will also be less effective at design. Design and manufacturing must be closely linked in order to produce the most cost effective products. A number of multi-national companies are now doing more of their product design work in foreign countries where the products are being manufactured for this reason as well for lower costs. These companies recognize the close interrelationship between design and manufacturing. As foreign countries improve their education and design capabilities, many more products will be both designed and manufactured overseas. As this trend continues, it will also cost the U.S. more higher paying professional jobs as well as further diminish our 'know how'.

Economic Growth
Economic globalization has shifted economic growth from developed countries like the U.S. to developing countries. Many of the developing countries have been experiencing economic growth rates two to three times that of developed countries.

The Chinese economy has grown at an annual compounded rate (on a per capita basis) as follows:

Period	China GDP Growth
1980-1990	212.0%
1990-2000	209.4%
2000-2014	342.1%

(The World Bank IBRD-IDA, 2015)

During the period from1980 to 2014, the U.S. economy grew by 75.7%, or from $28,957 per capita GDP to $50,902, compared to an overall growth rate of 416.9% for China, or over five times that of the U.S.

Much of the Chinese growth was 'catch-up growth', as the Chinese economy started from a very low base compared to that of the U.S. However, China is rapidly reaching the point where it is doing as well as the U.S. in a number of industries, and even surpassing the U.S. in some fields such as high-speed rail, solar energy, and nuclear energy. (About News, 2015)

During the last decade, China became the second largest economy in the world behind the U.S. China has also begun to build both physical and intellectual infrastructure for continued long-term economic growth. This Chinese economic growth story is being repeated in other developing countries, such as Hong Kong, Singapore, South Korea, Vietnam, and Poland.

Winners and Losers
The major winners from economic globalization over the past several decades have been the developing countries, and the millions of their citizens who now have

a better life economically, and good prospects for continued improvement for the next generations.

The losers in economic terms have been many citizens of primarily developed countries who now have fewer opportunities to improve their economic position, and in many cases even to maintain their position.

As many developing countries lifted their citizens out of poverty, the U.S. and some other developed countries now have a higher percentage of their citizens living in poverty than several decades ago. The unemployment and poverty rates have both increased in a number of developed countries. Current unemployment rates in many European countries as an example are in excess of 25%.

Bright Spots
A positive consequence for some Americans of economic globalization is increased employment opportunities in the U.S. There are new jobs available in ocean and air shipping, trucking, rail transportation, warehousing, distribution, outsourcing, and logistics. Many of these jobs are high paying, and some do not require a four-year college degree. A recent transportation and logistics industry report indicated that:

- Transportation and materials handling careers are up 15 percent, and will create 1.3 million new positions.
- Retail trade logistics employment is up 12 percent, and will create more than 1.8 million new jobs.

- Transportation and warehousing is up by 20 percent, and will generate 853,000 new jobs.
- Overall, high-level logistics management employment will increase by a modest projection of seven percent within the next seven years. (Batchelor, 2015)

Those who pursue careers in these fields can benefit from the growth of economic globalization.

Global Higher Education
As the world becomes more globally connected, there is a freer movement of students around the world. More students from many different countries are deciding to study abroad.

There were 886,052 foreign students studying at American colleges and universities for the 2013-2014 academic year. This represented 4.4% of the total number of foreign students in the world, and an increase of 72% in foreign studying in the U.S. since 2000.

The leading home countries for students studying in the U.S. are: China, India, and South Korea. Together these countries represent about half of all foreign students in the U.S. (Haynie, 2014)

More U.S. students are studying abroad as well. In the 2012-2013 academic year, 283,332 American college students studied in foreign countries; but this represents less than 1% of the total number of Americans attending colleges and universities. (NAFSA, 2015)

U.S. colleges and universities are benefiting with the additional revenues from foreign students studying in America. Typically foreign students attending U.S.

colleges and universities pay from 1.5 to 2.0 times as much as U.S. students studying in the same institutions. The increase in the number of foreign students attending American colleges and universities has been a growing source of additional revenues for U.S. higher education.

Students from foreign countries who study in the U.S. gain knowledge in fields such as engineering, science, medicine, computer technology, and business. They can take this knowledge back to their home countries and contribute to improving their economy and standard of living.

U.S. students studying in the U.S. also benefit from foreign students studying in America by getting exposure to a variety of different cultures in both an academic setting and a social setting. This exposure can better prepare American students to deal with diversity and to work more effectively in multi-national companies.

American students who study abroad also benefit from exposure to other countries and their cultures. They gain a better understanding of cultural differences, as well as a better understanding of the global economy.

As the developing countries set up their own centers of higher education, often in partnership with major U.S. and European universities, the financial benefits to U.S. institutions of higher education may decline over time.

World Poverty
A very positive effects of world economic globalization has been the growth in the size of the middle class in many developing countries. Especially in Asia, globalization has led to improved standards of living for many of its citizens. Millions of people in developing

countries such as China, Vietnam, India, and South Korea have been lifted out of poverty and now enjoy a richer and more fulfilling life as a result.

The Economist reported that between 1981 and 2001 China lifted 680 million of its citizens out of poverty. This represents about half of China's population. In 1980, 84% of China's population suffered from extreme poverty, today it is less than 10%.

From 1990 to 2010 the world poverty rate declined from 43% of world population to 21%. Almost all of the decrease can be attributed to economic growth, fueled by globalization. It is estimated that over one billion people have now been lifted out of poverty, or about 15% of the world's population. (The Economist, 2013)

More Winners and Losers
Major winners from economic globalization have been those countries and their citizens who have experienced rapid economic growth. Their economic growth has led to higher employment levels in manufacturing, construction, health care, mining, and technology for millions of their citizens, and a stronger and more self-reliant economy for the countries.

Some of the losers from global economic globalization have been some citizens of developed countries who had been employed in industries that have shrunk in size as a result of the transfer of work to other countries.

The benefits of economic globalization to developing countries may not be long-lasting. As their standard of living and education improve, costs tend to increase. Work is then transferred to yet other developing countries with lower costs. Some of the low cost garment manufacturing has recently moved from China to Vietnam and Bangladesh as China's manufacturing costs have increased. In the world's continuing pursuit of lower costs in the global economy, there is less economic stability.

Global Debt
The growth of government debt is becoming a major world concern. Total debt relative to GDP for developed countries is now in excess of 300%, compared to around 280% in 2000.

A number of countries such as Greece, Italy, Japan, and Spain are borrowing at an increasing rate to meet current obligations or in attempts to stimulate their economies. These countries and others have failed to implement sufficient reforms to slow the trend of increasing debt levels. As global economic growth slows and interest rates increase, there is increased risk of defaults, resulting in the loss of confidence in the global financial system, and perhaps leading to another financial crisis. (The Economist, 2015)

The Bottom Line
As the world economic system moved from a national and regional basis to economic globalization, there have been winners and loser.

Some winners are:

- **Businesses won** by gaining access to lower cost materials and labor from anywhere in the world, and access to world markets for their products and services. This has led to their growth in both revenues and profits. Many U.S. companies now get over half of their annual revenues from overseas activities.

- **Developing countries won** by receiving investments of foreign capital to develop infrastructure and industries, creating more and higher paying jobs. This has improved the overall economy of many developing countries and has lifted millions of its citizens out of poverty. The growth in foreign currency reserves from exports has improved the financial strength of many developing countries as well.
- **Consumers won** as they have gained access to a greater variety of products and services from anywhere in the world at lower costs.
- **Students** who are willing to study in fields that have application on a global basis, and who are willing to re-locate to other parts of the world can take advantage of the growing opportunities in many global professions.
- **The World won** by a reduction in the number of people in the world who are living in poverty, as there are many more people who are self-sufficient rather than dependent on foreign aid and charities for their basic needs.

Some losers include:

- **The U.S. and other developed countries lost** as many are experiencing lower rates of economic growth, growing negative trade balances, loss of expertise in basic manufacturing and other technologies, and fewer lower and middle income good paying jobs.

- **Many U.S. Citizens lost** as many had depended on manufacturing and support jobs, and now have fewer opportunities to earn a good living.
- **The United States lost** as U.S. companies made more investments in foreign countries and less in the U.S. Offshoring increasingly reduces the number of job opportunities for Americans. As the negative balance of trade grows, the U.S. transfers more wealth and control of its economy and finances to foreign countries.

How we as individuals deal with the global economy depends on our understanding of what the current situation is, and our assessment of our options within the global economic system.

If we have better information about the impact of economic globalization, we are better prepared to make the best choices that enable us to have the life that we want.

It is unlikely that the world will revert to the way it was several generations ago and reverse the negative impacts of economic globalization. We need to accept today's reality and find ways to achieve our goals in today's global economy.

Let's now look more specifically at the U.S. economy to see what some of the major issues are that we have to navigate through to have the fulfilling life we are seeking in America.

Chapter 4
Our Economy

We will begin our review of the U.S. economy with some facts about its size and scope.

Size and Scope

The United States' economy is the world's largest, representing 17% of total global GDP. The U.S. GDP is estimated to be $17. 7 trillion in 2015. The Chinese economy is now the world's second largest at $10.3 trillion. Some economists predict that by 2020 the size of the Chinese economy will surpass that of the U.S.

The U.S. has had abundant natural resources, a well-developed infrastructure, a high level of innovation, and high labor productivity.

Today the U.S. infrastructure is aged and in need of major repair and upgrading. Funding for infrastructure maintenance and upgrading has declined in the past decade. Productivity gains in the U.S. have slowed to a rate of about one half the long-run historical average. Government spending on research and development has slowed in the past two decades.

Currently the U.S. has the 10th highest per capita GDP of all countries; and the fourth highest median household income, down from second highest in 2000.

The U.S. has one of the largest and most influential financial markets in the world. The New York Stock Exchange is the world's largest financial market as measured by market capitalization.

Foreign investments in the U.S. total about $2.65 trillion, and U.S. investment in foreign countries are over $4.45 trillion.

Business and Trade
The U.S. is the second largest trading nation in the world behind China, and the second largest manufacturer, with about one fifth of total global manufacturing output.

128 of the world's 500 largest companies or 25.8% are headquartered in the U.S.

Consumer spending represents about 72% of the total U.S. economy, and the U.S. represents the largest consumer market in the world.

11.3% of U.S. workers are now represented by labor unions, the lowest rate of all OECD nations, and down from 33.9% in the 1950's. (Office of Management and Budget, 2011)

Poverty
Households living on less than $2 per day (before government benefits) doubled from 1996 to 2011 to 1.5 million. The gap between the rich and the poor (income inequality) is greater in the U.S. than in any other developed country.

Debt
Total public and private debt is almost $60 trillion, or 3.5 times GDP, up from about $53 trillion in 2010, and $28 trillion in 2000.

Public-sector spending now represents 30% of GDP up from 28% in 1998, and far from the historical rate of 4% of

GDP prior to the 1960's (except for brief periods of wars and financial crises).

Total Federal Government debt now stands at $17.1 trillion or 107% of GDP.

Government Spending

Federal Government departments with the largest expenditures are:

Department	% of Total Budget
Health & Human Services	24.6%
Social Security Admin	21.8%
Defense	18.8%
Treasury	15.0%

(Office of Management and Budget, 2011)

These four departments in total represents over 80% of all Federal Government spending.

With the aging U.S. population, the two largest expenditure categories (Health and Human Services and Social Security) are projected to continue to increase over the next several decades.

Consumption

The economy of the U.S. is highly dependent on consumption. Currently about 72% of total GDP in the U.S. is made up of the consumption of goods and services. The rate of consumption has **increased from 62% of GDP in 1960.**

The rate of consumption in the U.S. compares to 61.1% for Japan, 34.1% for China, 64.6% for the United Kingdom, 62.6% for Brazil, 55.9% for Germany, 46.1% for

Ireland, 37.7% for Singapore, 60.9% for Poland, and 55.0% for Australia. No other major economy has as high a rate of consumption than the U.S. (Bank, 2015)

This high rate of consumption in the U.S. means that other segments of the economy, such as savings and investment, receive very little. This over-consumption hurts long-term economic development as well as personal financial security. Americans are using most all of their income on spending for today, and very little, if any, for savings and the future.

Personal Savings
The personal savings rate in the U.S. went from about 10% of income in the late 1970's to a negative rate in the 1990's and 2000's. Personal borrowing has increased significantly during this period to support continued high rates of personal consumption, in the face of declining real incomes for the lower and middle class. This lack of personal savings weakens the financial security of Americans, and provides little for personal investments. 45% of the working households in the U.S. have no retirement savings. Among those who do, the median retirement account balance is less than $60.000. 76% of Americans are living from paycheck to paycheck, and 43.9% of Americans have no savings at all. (Johnson, 2013)

Personal Debt
As of July, 2015, the average household credit card debt in the U.S. was $7,400. If those households who have no credit card debt are excluded, the average for those who have debt would be $15,863. The average household mortgage debt is $156,584; and the average student loan debt is $33,090.

As of July 1, 2015, total American indebtedness was $11.86 billion, an increase of 8.5% from 2014. (Chen, 2015)

High levels of consumer debt add monthly interest expenses to households, and further limits their ability to save. The average person with a $4,000 credit card balance pays about $700 per year in interest and penalties. If credit card balances could be paid monthly, this savings in interest and penalties, could be the start of a retirement savings plan for millions of Americans.

Innovation
One of the drivers of the U.S. economy has been the inventiveness of its citizens, and the willingness of business and government to invest in research and development. The U.S. was the home of 161 of the 321 greatest inventions as listed by *Encyclopedia Britannica*. This represents over 50% of all great inventions.

The Federal Government has historically been an important source of funds for research and development. The Federal Government has provided both direct funding through grants, as well as its own research programs and facilities. The Federal Government has also provided funds for research and development through tax credits and special tax treatment for research and development expenditures for businesses.

With recent increases in funds required for social programs, government funding for research and development has declined. Federal funding of R&D is now lower as a percent of GDP, and as a percent of the federal budget than it was two decades ago.

Innovation has been the source of many new industries and jobs in the U.S. and the source of productivity improvements, both of which have contributed to Americas' increased standard of living.

The internet, that we now take for granted, and GPS systems which guide us in our travels, are both the result of Federal Government investments in research and development. Our space program is another very successful national R&D program funded by the federal government.

A reduction in federal funding for R&D creates a risk that the U.S. will no longer be a leader in innovation. This is particularly true today, as we compete in a global economy.

A Diverse Economy
The U.S. economy has been broad-based and very diverse. This has allowed the U.S. to meet all of is needs from food (agriculture) and energy (mining), to capital for investments (finance), and all consumer products (manufacturing).

Today the U.S. economy is not as diverse nor self-sufficient as it was in the 1950's and 1960's. The chart below shows what the U.S. economy looks like today in terms of percent of GDP value added for various economic sectors.

Industry	% GDP
All governments	14%
Real estate and Leasing	13%
Manufacturing	12%
Health Care	8%
Finance and Insurance	8%
Retail Trade	6%
Wholesale Trade	6%
Information Technology	4%
Arts and Entertainment	4%
Construction	4%
Waste Services	3%
Other Services	3%
Utilities	2%
Mining	2%
Corporate Management	2%
Educational Services	1%
Agriculture	1%

(Industry GDP, 2012)

This data highlights how government and service oriented the U.S. economy has become. All of the sectors from the above chart that are service or service-related industries represent 68% of total GDP, manufacturing, mining, and construction represents 18%, and government represents 14%. This means that only 18% of the total U.S. economy represents production activities.

In 1950, 48% of private sector employment in the U.S. was in manufacturing. By 2010, manufacturing employment had declined to 18%. Today it is 9%. Service industries now represent over 80% of private sector employment. (Johnson L. D., 2012)

Employment

There are approximately 154.4 million workers in the U.S. Governments (Federal, state and local) employ the largest number at 22 million or 14% of the total workforce.

Small business is the largest overall employer group, employing 53% of all U.S. workers. Large businesses employ 38% of the U.S. workforce. Walmart is the largest private sector employer in the U.S. with 1.4 million employees in the U.S., and a total of 2.1 million world-wide.

The 30 million small businesses in the U.S. accounted for 70% of all new jobs created in the U.S. in the past decade. (WikipediA, Economy of the United States, 2015)

Income Inequality

From 2009 to 2011 the top 1% of income earners in the U.S. accounted for 95% of income gains. Their share of total U.S. income has more than doubled, from 9% in 1976 to 20% in 2011.

According to a 2014 OECD (Organization for Economic Cooperation and Development) report, from 1975 to 2007 (just prior to the financial crisis), 80% of total income growth in the U.S. went to the top 10%. The top 10% now have 80% of all financial assets in the U.S. Wealth inequity in the U.S. is now greater than all developed countries in the world except Switzerland and Denmark.

The wealthiest 10% of Americans control 75% of total American wealth. This leaves only 25% of total wealth for the other 75% of Americans.

By 2010 the U.S. had the fourth widest income distribution (income inequity) behind only Turkey, Mexico and Chile. The U.S. also has great inequality in wealth distribution.

In his recent book, *Average is Over*, Tyler Cowen points out that there are now more rich people and more poor people in this country than ever before. The U.S. middle class is getting smaller. The rich make up 1% of the population but represent 35.6% of all the wealth in the U.S. (Cowen, Average is Over, 2013)

Middle Class jobs
Many routine middle-class jobs have been eliminated with automation, corporate restructuring, and offshoring. Almost all business sectors now rely less on labor and more on automation and other forms of technology. Robotics have replaced many workers such as assemblers, welders, and other historically high paying production jobs. Many traditional labor jobs have been moved overseas to lower costs.

As a consequence of the combination of automation and offshoring, 75% of the jobs created since the recession of 2008 pay $13.52 an hour or less. These new jobs have been primarily in retail, leisure, and hospitality. Traditional middle-class jobs have rapidly disappeared from the U.S. economy.

Productivity
From the onset of the Industrial Revolution in the mid 1800's, businesses in the U.S. have experienced growth in productivity, which has resulted in a higher standard of living for all Americans for many decades. Gains in productivity were shared amongst the company shareholders, the government, and workers. All

participants in the U.S. economy benefited from gains in productivity.

In automobile manufacturing, Henry Ford introduced innovations such as the moving assembly line, parts standardization, standard work methods, and employee training. As a result of these productivity improvements, the cost of the Model T decreased from $850 in 1908 to less than $300 by1925. During this period, Henry Ford doubled the wages of his workers to $5 per day. Both management and labor shared in the gains.

With the sharing of productivity gains with Ford workers, many workers could afford to buy cars. This increase in demand helped to fuel the growth of the automobile industry. The Model T represented over 40% of all the cars sold during that time. This is one of many examples of the economic benefit of sharing productivity gains with workers. It is good for business, the workers, and the overall economy. Everyone wins.

Between the years of 1891 and 2007, the productivity in the U.S. grew at an average annual rate of over 2%.

Since 2007 the U.S. economy has experienced a decline in the rate of productivity growth to a current level of around 1%. Many economists believe that this trend is likely to continue as the U.S. transitions its economy to more retail, personal services, health care, and other knowledge work and away from the production of goods. Productivity gains are more difficult to achieve in service related industries. (Wilson, June 2002)

Underlying the decline in the rate of productivity gains in the U.S. is slower growth of the U.S. economy, lower investments in U.S. businesses, and an increasing shift to more importing of both products and services. This current trend of lower than historical productivity gains does not bode well for the average American, as productivity improvements had helped offset stagnant real incomes by giving workers more buying power with the same income as prices declined with productivity improvements. (Binder, 2015)

An increasing amount of U.S. corporate profits are coming as a result of outsourcing, and not from improvements made in the U.S. If this trend continues, then the standard of living for many Americans will likely decline, especially in light of the fact that these corporate profit improvements coming from overseas operations are not broadly shared with U.S. workers.

Incomes
Since the year 1974, there has been a growing divergence in the relationship between the rates of productivity improvement and increases in worker's incomes in the U.S. Prior to this time, productivity improvements had been shared between business and worker. As productivity improved, employee wages and/or benefits increased in about the same proportion.

Since 1999 real (inflation adjusted) median family incomes have been flat to declining, while economic productivity continued to improve. Since 1947 overall productivity in the U.S. has increased about 300% while real median family incomes have increased by only about 110%.

In real terms, median household incomes are lower than they were in 1989 and only 11% higher than in 1970. Further evidence that many middle class American households are not better off economically than they were twenty-five years ago. (The Economist, 2015)

Since 1999 businesses have taken an increased percentage of economic productivity gains. This is reflected both in the increases in executive compensation relative to worker's wages, and in the increased share of corporate profits as a percent of GDP. U.S. workers in general are getting a smaller piece of the economic pie. In the long-run this trend is harmful to both workers and to business. If workers have less income, they will not be able to buy as much, thus reducing the incomes of businesses. This trend has already begun in the U.S.

Employment
As of February 2013, the distribution of U.S. workers by industry group was:

Industry	% of total employment
Retail	10%
Education	10%
Health Care	9%
Food Service	8%
Professional Services	6%
Admin & Waste Services	5%
Finance and Insurance	4%
Construction	4%
Manufacturing	4%

(2012 Statistical Abstract: Labor Force, Employment and Earnings)

The table shows that many of the industries where a large percentages of workers are employed are in lower paying service industries, such as retail, food services, and some education and health care.

The U.S. economy has been creating many more low-paying service jobs in the past decade than high paying professional, technical, or manufacturing jobs. As previously mentioned, manufacturing continues to employ a smaller percentage of the total workforce in the U.S.

Poverty

According to recent U.S. census data, half the U.S. population is either low income or lives in poverty. Four out of five American adults struggle with joblessness or near-poverty, and rely on some form of welfare for at least part of their lives.

The current poverty line for an individual is defined as an income less than $11,490 per year for a single individual, and for a family of four, an income of less than $23,550. Today, over 45 million Americans live below the poverty line (before government benefits), or 14.5% of the U.S. population. A third of single women with children, or 15.6 million, live in poverty. One in three children in the U.S. lives in poverty. (Gongloff, 2014)

Health Care

The U.S. spends more on health care than any other country in the world as measured in terms of total dollars spent, percentage of GDP, and per capita. A high level of health care spending does not necessarily result in better health. The U.S. has a lower average life expectancy than many other countries who spend much less on health care.

According to the World Health Organization (WHO), the U.S. spends $7,146 per person on health care, which is a total of 15.2% of GDP. This amounts to over $3 trillion per year. With its aging population, and increased access to health care through The Patient Protection and Affordable Care Act (Obama Care), U.S. expenditures on health care are expected to continue to rise over the next several decades. Health care is also now the largest single government expenditure.

The high cost of health care in the U.S. can be attributed to a number of factors. They include:

- a high level of fraud in the health care industry
- technological advances that increase cost
- high health care industry administrative costs
- drug pricing policies that manage high pricing
- governmental regulations
- health care lobbying in Washington
- high wages of doctors and other health care professionals
- the poor health of Americans (obesity and other life-style issues)
- an emphasis on cures and extending life, rather than on finding root causes and prevention
- litigation and the resultant high cost of liability insurance
- high advertising expenditures by the pharmaceutical industry to direct 'sell' the consumer on using more pharmaceuticals
- additional and often unnecessary testing procedures by medical professionals

In the U.S. 20-25% of all health care costs are incurred in the last six months of a person's life, often to extend life with poor quality of living and for a short period of time.

According to the World Health Organization (based on 2013 data), the U.S. ranked 34th in the world in average life expectancy. The average life expectancy in the U.S. is now 79 years, with American males at 76 years and females at 81 years. This is the same as Cuba, Columbia and Costa Rica, all of whom spend much less on health care per capita than the U.S.

Japan has the highest average life expectancy at 84 years, followed by Australia, Switzerland, Italy and Singapore, all at 83 years.

The quality of life for many U.S. seniors is not as good as it is in other countries with similar longevities, Many American seniors suffer from chronic diseases, and as a result, are on medications and other life supporting regimens. They therefore are not able to fully enjoy their final years.

The U.S. health care system is not giving Americans good value for dollars spent, and will continue to be a financial drain on more Americans, especially the middle-class and the elderly. With health care expenditures projected to increase over the next several decades, the financial burden on both individuals and the government will only increase.

Trade
In 2013 trade represented 29.8% of all U.S. economic activity. Imports of goods and services were $2.74 trillion or 16.3% of GDP. Exports were $2.29 trillion. The trade deficit for the U.S. in 2013 was $450.3 billion.

The largest trading partners for the U.S. have been Canada, China, Mexico, Japan, Germany, the U.K., South Korea, France, Taiwan, and Brazil.

According to the U.S. Bureau of Census data, the U.S. balance of trade deficit has grown from $80.9 billion in 1990, to $372.5 billion in 2000, and to $508.3 billion in 2014. The last year that the U.S. had a positive balance of trade was in 1975. The U.S. continues to purchase more goods and services from foreign countries than it sells to them, thus continuing to transfer U.S. wealth to foreign countries. This continuing annual foreign trade deficit gives foreign countries more control over the U.S. economy, its currency, and its finances. There are limits to how large the U.S. balance of trade deficit can get before there are detrimental effects on the U.S. economy. These limits are unknown as this level of trade deficits has not occurred before.

Economic Growth
Over the past two decades, the growth rate of the total output of goods and services (GDP) of the U.S. has declined from its long-term trend. This decline in economic growth has been due primarily to the recession of 2008, the growth of imports, and the transition of the U.S. economy from manufacturing to service and knowledge.

The growth of the U.S. economy went from an average annual rate of 4.0% in 1995-1999; to a low of 0.94% for the period of 2005-2009 (affected by the recession), to a current rate of 2.2% for the period of 2010-2014. (The World Bank, 2015)

The slower growth rate of the U.S. economy has resulted in slower growth in employment and in a smaller percentage of adults both working and looking for work.

Fewer Working Americans

The U.S. is currently experiencing a reduction in labor force participation rate. This statistic measures the percentage of those of working age (19-64) who are actually working. The measure includes full-time employment, part-time employment, and self-employment.

As of June 2015 the U.S. labor force participation rate was 62.6%, the lowest level since 1977. In 2000 it peaked at 67.3%.

The impact of this drop in workforce participation rate is significant on the U.S. economy, and the standard of living for many Americans. If the labor force participation rate today was at the peak of 2000, there would be an additional 11.3 million Americans in the workforce. If they were looking for jobs, the U.S. unemployment rate would be 13%, rather than the currently reported rate of 5.2%. If we do not look at unemployment figures together with the workforce participation rate, we are not reflecting an accurate or complete picture of the employment conditions in the U.S.

In June of 2015 alone, 432,000 Americans dropped out of the workforce. This is an indication that the workforce participation rate continues to decline, and that we are understating the unemployment statistics.

Factors that have contributed to the decline in the workforce participation rate are the lack of sufficient job creation, and the lack of skilled workers to fill the positions being created by technology. Many good paying jobs are going unfilled as there are not enough qualified candidates.

If the trend of declining workforce participation rates continue, it will further restrict the future growth of the U.S. economy, and put increasing demands on the government to supply basic needs to its citizens. Fewer Americans will be supporting more. (Shilling, 2015)

Many Americans who are of working age and physically able to work, are not working for a variety of reasons. Some cannot find the type of job they want, some are full-time students, some are raising children, some lack the training or skills for available jobs, and some are claiming government benefits that are greater than if they worked. The higher the percentage of the workforce that is actually working is a measure of the health and growth potential of the economy.

During most of the 1990's, the labor force participation rate in the U.S. was over 67%. In the 1950's and 1960's, of men between the ages of 25-64 (considered the prime working years), only 9% were not working. Today that figure exceeds 18%. In the 1980's during the recession only about 15% of men in that category were not working.

This condition of an increase in the number of men in their prime working years not working does not bode well for family incomes, especially for the middle class. Most of these men in the 1950's and 1960's were working in relatively high paying middle class jobs. These are the jobs that are no longer being created in large numbers by our economy, and if fact are declining.

As further evidence of the lack of good paying jobs for the American working male, between 1969 and 2009, median wages for male workers have fallen about 28%.

The Bottom Line
The U.S. economy continues to be the largest in the world. China, if it continues on its current growth path, may take over the lead within the next decade.

Since the industrial revolution, the U.S. has been a world leader in innovation, per capita income, economic productivity, and standard of living for all its citizens. The last two decades have seen a decline in these metrics.

Today the U.S. economy is less diverse. The U.S. economy and its citizens have become more dependent on imported goods and services, at the expense of the loss of many high paying manufacturing jobs, the loss of manufacturing expertise, and the loss of economic self-sufficiency.

In the past several decades U.S. productivity growth has slowed. Imports have far outstripped exports, resulting in a growing negative balance of trade. Businesses are taking a larger share of the productivity and profit improvements than workers, limiting the income growth potential of many Americans.

More Americans have become dependent on government financial support and government services.

The percentage of GDP for both government expenditures and personal consumption has increased.

Both savings and investment have decreased in the U.S. over the past several decades. Consumer debt continues to increase, putting more Americans at greater financial risk, and not adequately preparing them for a secure retirement.

The federal budget deficit has grown, as government expenditures continue to outpace tax revenues.

The U.S. is devoting an increasing share of GDP on health care; taking resources away from other sectors of the economy, and increasing the financial burden on the lower and middle class Americans.

The income inequality gap, and the concentration of wealth have both increased, resulting in a declining size of middle class, and pushing more Americans into poverty.

A smaller percentage of the U.S. workforce is actually working, putting more burden on government and those who are working. The U.S. economy has lost many higher paying middle-class jobs and replaced them with lower paying service jobs. More Americans are living in poverty or near poverty.

Government and private industry investments in infrastructure, business development and R&D in the U.S. has declined as a percent of GDP; investments in foreign countries has increased.

Based on the current state of the U.S. economy, the current generation and the next, will be more challenged to find ways to have the standard of living and life style that the last several generations have enjoyed.

With the high level of overall debt in the U.S., America is vulnerable to additional shocks to its economy. In the past several decades we have lost some control of both our personal and our economic destiny.

Let's now look at how business, particularly U.S. corporations may have contributed to some of the economic issues that the U.S. is currently facing.

Chapter 5
Our Business Environment

Based on a series of recent polls taken in the U.S. over the past several years, many Americans feel that corporate America and Wall Street are not working in the best interests of America or the American worker.

There were a number of anti-business issues that received increased attention by the press in the past several years which subsequently led to the failed Occupy Wall Street protest movement in 2013-2014.

Some of the issues that created anti-business sentiment, particularly among the younger generation included: increasingly higher corporate profits, growing disparity between executive compensation and that of wage earners, an increasing number of corporate ethical lapses, continuing offshoring of manufacturing, service, and knowledge jobs, an increase in corporate lobbying, the decline of corporate investment in the U.S., financial engineering creating 'paper wealth, and short-term corporate thinking to maximize profits.

Many Americans feel that corporate leaders in the U.S, have only their own best interests in mind. U.S. corporate leaders are seen by many Americans as using their employees, their customers, the government, and their power, to accomplish their single objective of maximizing profits. Many Americans are concerned that U.S. corporate leadership has lost their commitment to their employees as well as to the long-term best interests of America.

Let's look at the facts surrounding these feelings and concerns, and attempt to determine what is real, what is significant, and what might impact our future.

Social Responsibility
Many Americans hold the view that U.S. corporations should not focus solely on maximizing profits. Corporations have a responsibility to balance the needs of shareholders (profits and growth) with the needs of other stakeholders. This broader role of corporate responsibility beyond maximizing profits for shareholders is referred to as 'corporate social responsibility'.

When corporate decisions are made, consideration must be given to the potential impact on employees, suppliers, local communities, the environment, government, and customers. Corporations do not operate in a vacuum, but are members of a larger community and society, and therefore have responsibilities to those who make up that community, as well as to their shareholders.

Mark Mizruchi, in his book, *The Fracturing of the American Corporate Elite*, points out that there has been a major shift in the emphasis by U.S. corporate executives to short-term profits and away from accepting their social responsibility. This corporate focus on profits is more of a traditional shareholder perspective rather than the broader stakeholder perspective, and was very prevalent during the period of the early industrialization of the U.S. and prior to the 1929 Recession.

After WWII, American business leaders practiced an 'ethic of civic responsibility and enlightened self-interest.'

They accepted organized labor and supported federal regulation of the economy. Corporate leaders recognized and accepted that they had to consider broader society's needs and just not that of the shareholders. During this period there was a balance between the needs of business, the worker, and government.

Mizruchi points out that in the 1970's, corporate leadership began to change their view on social responsibility, and began to focus on shareholder value and short-term profit gains, rather than the long-term issues facing the country at the time. Corporate leaders became more focused on corporate performance and less about the impacts on other stakeholders. (Mizruchi, 2013)

As continued today by U.S. corporate leadership, their narrow focus on shareholders and short-term profits, has caused damage to our economy. The single focus on growth of short-term profits, has recently led to increased intervention of government into business through increased regulation and oversight, and has resulted in the loss of millions of jobs in the U.S. as the world suffered through the Global Financial Crisis.

Business and Government
In spite of increased governmental regulation and oversight of business, businesses have become increasingly more influential with the federal government regarding new legislation and regulations. This undue corporate influence has often led to legislation that favors the business goal of maximizing profits. Much of this business influenced legislation has

been detrimental to the interests of workers and to the nation as a whole.

The Patient Protection and Affordable Care Act (aka Obama Care) is an example of undue corporate influence on federal legislation. This bill was greatly influenced, and partially written by the health insurance companies, pharmaceutical companies, medical professionals, and medical equipment manufacturers. The consumers of health care had little input into the legislative process. As a result, the legislation favors the health care industry at the expense of the consumer in many aspects.

In his book, *America's Bitter Pill,* Steven Brill shows how all of the health care industry groups worked to assure that their interests were heard and incorporated into the final legislation. In the drafting of the Patient Protection and Affordable Care Act, deals were made between the government and the healthcare providers to protect their interests (and profits); and often at the expense of the consumer. (Brill, America's Bitter Pill, 2015)

Many other examples of legislation influenced by special interest business groups, shows a strong link between government and business for the benefit of business. There is much less representation for the average American in the legislative process, as consumers do not have the organization or the resources to mount an effective counter attack and have their voices heard.

The Three-legged Stool
From the end of WWII up to the 1970's, there was a degree of balance between the interests of

government, business, and the worker. I describe this as the 'Three Legged Stool':

1. Government
2. Business
3. The Worker

The three legs were in balance so that no one leg had undue influence on the others, and the stool was strong and could foster a strong economy where all interests were represented. The 'three-legged stool' could stand and withhold the weight of normal disruptions to the economy, as there was balance. All three legs, government, business, and workers, accepted the fact that they were dependent on each other, and all had to be strong and support the U.S. economy together. This acceptance of interdependence of the three parties made our businesses in a free economy work.

During the period following WWII most workers were represented by organized labor unions. This representation provided workers with a unified voice to influence management on decisions regarding working conditions, pay, and benefits.

U.S. companies were very dependent on their workforce, as they had limited options at that time. Management was compelled to negotiate with labor unions for wages, working conditions, and benefits. Outsourcing and moving production to lower cost countries was not a common practice then. Therefore, management worked to maintain good working relations with workers and their unions.

As a result of labor negotiations, workers were able to get their 'fair share' of productivity gains and keep corporate greed in check. During the period from after WWII up to the 1970's, workers enjoyed steady growth in real income, and an increase in benefits, which provided an improvement in their standard of living.

As the world became more global, and U.S. corporate management faced foreign competition, corporate management began to look for ways to lower costs. Options such as relocating production to lower cost areas of the U.S., offshoring to lower cost countries, or importing components for products, were some of the options that U.S. companies considered, and began to implement.

The movement of production to the lower cost non-union south in the U.S. and to Mexico, was the first step in the process of reducing labor costs, and neutralizing the power of labor unions. This movement of production began the de-industrialization of America. With continued offshoring, most of the standard manufactured items that Americans buy today are no longer made in the U.S., or if they are, they are made in much smaller volumes with the majority coming from other countries.

As the U.S. economy transitioned from a manufacturing economy to a service and knowledge economy, fewer workers were represented by labor unions, and workers began to lose their voice in business decisions. Only a small percentage of service workers are represented by labor unions. As a result of lower costs, and the lack of worker representation, corporate profit margins increased, executive compensation increased, and corporate foreign investments increased, all at the cost of jobs and corporate investments in the U.S.

Today workers have much less influence over what corporations pay them and what benefits they receive. This is a contributing factor to the flat and declining real earnings of the middle class in the U.S. over the past decade. Today only 11% of all workers are represented by labor unions, with the largest number in the public sector.

In a number of other countries, public corporations are required to have representatives of workers as members on the board of directors so that their needs are considered in corporate decisions.

The second leg of the three-legged stool, government, was considerably weakened, at the time that business and special interests lobbying became a major influence on legislation in Washington. The Federal Government often favored the interests of business in legislation more than it did the interests of the consumer or the worker.

Businesses now spend billions of dollars each year attempting to influence legislation and even write legislation so that they will get the most favorable treatment. The worker or the average American has little or no voice in this process.

As a result of the pharmaceutical manufacturers lobbying and involvement in the Medicare Modernization Act of 2003, it has been estimated that the industry will gain benefits of $242 billion over a ten year period.

The American Jobs Creation Act of 2004, which was aimed at cutting foreign imports, resulted in big handouts for business.

With the closer linking of government and business, and the concurrent loss of influence of workers, the three-legged stool became a one-legged stool, with government and business linked, and the worker or average American citizen being basically shut out of the process.

Lobbyists

According to a recent report in *The Economist*, in 2012 business lobbyists in Washington accounted for more than 75% of the $3.3 billion spent on lobbying Washington. Besides direct lobbyists, businesses employ others that attempt to influence the government such as 'government relations' personnel, 'public affairs' personnel, and 'corporate communications' personnel.

Business lobbying has become a very large and powerful institution in Washington. Lobbyists are involved in many aspects of government's work in Washington to assure that their interests are heard and satisfied. One of the major ways that business lobbyists influence legislation is in the drafting of bills.

Recent studies suggest that corporations have gone from using lobbyists to protect themselves from legislation that might have a negative impact on their industry, to using politics to help them become more profitable. (Schumpter, 2015)

A recent example of how U.S. corporations lobby for their own benefit and not for the common good, is when the Coca-Cola Corporation, in conjunction with the food industry and farm lobbying groups, spent $15.3 million in the second quarter of 2015 to fight against a proposed government recommendation to cut U.S.

consumption of sugars and meat. Research has shown that the over consumption of these foods can lead to heart disease, diabetes and other life-style diseases. Proponents of the proposed governmental recommendations were only able to spend $1.1 million to fight giant Coca-Cola. (Chaussee, 2015)

In his book, *The Fracturing of The American Corporate Elite*, Mark Mizruchi states that U.S. corporations are now arguing through lobbyists for company or industry specific benefits, rather than for the common good.

Mizruchi also concludes that corporate lobbying is bad for America, as it often leads to gridlock in Congress. As evidence of the benefits of business lobbying, research has shown that companies who do extensive lobbying have lower corporate tax rates, and are less likely to be detected for fraud. (Mizruchi, 2013)

The work of Congress that should get done, such as improvement of infrastructure, simplifying the tax code, budget deficits, or dealing with immigration issues is impeded by lobbyists and often resultant gridlock.

Bribery
As they now have to compete on a world-wide basis, U.S. corporations are resorting to more unethical behaviors, such as bribery, to gain favor with foreign governments.

Several years ago, Wal-Mart was accused of bribing officials in the Mexican government in order to do business in Mexico on more favorable terms. Wal-Mart is projected to spend about $800 million on its internal investigation of this and other bribery concerns. Wal-Mart's bill for legal and accounting fees for the Mexican case alone will exceed $1 billion. This is just one of many examples of the increasing level of corporate bribery to gain favorable advantages in foreign countries.

The Economist recently reported that on a world-wide basis, there has been a significant increase in the amount of corporate bribery in the past ten years. As a result of the increase in bribery by U.S. corporations, there has been a significant increase in the amount of government money spent on investigation and litigation. This is another cost that society has to bear as a result of corporate abuse. (The Economist, 2015)

Executive Compensation

The amount of compensation that American corporate executives (CEO's and company presidents) receive has significantly increased relative to the earnings of workers over the past few decades. Corporate executives are getting a bigger piece of the corporate income pie, often at the expense of the workers.

> "From 1992 to 2005, median pay for chief executive officers in major U.S. companies rose 186%, while the median wage of all workers rose by 7%. In 2005, U.S. CEO's earned 262 times more than the average worker, whereas in 1965 they earned 25 times more." (Mather, 2008)

In 2013 executive pay was 331 times the average wage earner, and 774 times the minimum wage earner.

In other countries executive compensation is much less. Looking at data published in 2012:

- German CEO's received compensation of 147 times the average worker's pay;

- French CEO's receive 104 times;
- UK CEO's 84 times; and
- Japanese CEO's 67 times the average worker's pay. (Globalist, 2013)

In a recent review of the top 300 CEO's in the U.S. conducted by the Hay Group, and published by *The Wall Street Journal*, it was reported that the median compensation for this group of CEO's was $13.6 million; and there was not a consistent relationship between performance and pay.

A number of the CEO's had negative performance (as measured by shareholder return), and yet were compensated well.

A few examples of paying well for poor performance include:

- Steven Newman, CEO of Transocean, who earned $14.2 million in 2014 while the share value of the company dropped by 59.9%.
- Virginia Rometty, the CEO of IBM earned $19.3 million while the shares of IBM fell by 12.4%.
- Jeffery Immelt, the CEO of General Electric earned $37.3 million in 2014 while the share value of GE stock declined by 6.7%.
- Leslie Moonves, CEO of CBS earned $57.2 million in 2014 while the value of CBS shares declined by 12.4%.
- Philippe Dauman, the CEO of Viacom earned $44.3 million in 2014 while the shares of Viacom declined by 6.6%.

Many of these CEO's received increases in their compensation in 2014 even though the performance of their companies declined from the prior year.

The highest paid CEO in the study was Michael Fries, CEO of Liberty Global at $112.2 million; up 139% from 2013.

The median compensation in 2014 for CEO's in the survey increased by 13.5%, compared to an average increase in wages and salaries for all workers in the U.S. of 2.2%.

U.S. corporate executives are getting a bigger piece of the pie often irrespective of performance and the state of the general economy. (Lublin, 2015)

As a comparison, the President of the United States receives an annual salary of $400.000. He also receives a $50,000 expense allowance, a $100,000 travel allowance, and $19,000 for entertainment, or total compensation of $569,000. There are no stock options for the President of the United States as there are for corporate executives. Most Americans believe that it much harder to be the President of the United States, than to run an American corporation.

There are a few U.S. corporate leaders who believe that their compensation should be reasonable and not excessive. Warren Buffett, the founder and chairman of Berkshire Hathaway, one of the most successful corporations over the past 50 years, earns only $100,000 per year. Whole Foods, a very successful organic and natural food retailer, limits CEO pay to 19 times the average worker. These American corporate leaders are regretfully exceptions.

Health Insurance

An indication of how businesses continue focus on reducing costs at the expense of their employees, is how they are dealing with the costs of employer provided health insurance. Since 2005 the number of employees who are covered by employer provided health insurance has decreased by 3.5%, while the number of individuals providing their own health insurance increased by 25.4%. Some of this shift is due to an increase in the number of individuals who are self-employed. However, a number of employers are controlling the number of full- time workers they have in order to minimize the number of employees they are required to provide health insurance for. This is one of the negative consequences of Obama Care. (Weaver, 2015)

The Financial Crisis

Many books have been written in an attempt to explain the causes of the Global Financial Crisis of 2008. Most of these books fall short of explaining the root cause, which rest within the financial industry in the U.S. and its obsession with revenue and profit growth at any cost, and at anyone's expense.

What directly led to the Global Financial Crisis was the granting of mortgages to many households at artificially temporarily low payments and interests rates, without proper due diligence, and with little consideration given to the borrower's ability to pay. Many lenders and intermediaries knew that the borrowers could not afford the mortgage in the long run, but were influenced by corporate pressures and personal greed. After many of the mortgages were completed, they were 'packaged' and sold to unwary investors around the world as 'safe' high yielding investments. This process of easy and low costs mortgages for anyone who wanted one, rapidly and artificially drove up housing prices and fueled a speculative housing boom. This was the 'straw' that led to the collapse of an already over-leveraged global financial system.

Coupled with other Wall Street financial engineering creations such as derivatives, credit default swaps, hedge funds, and excessive leverage, the U.S. financial industry was building a financial 'sand castle' that would collapse under its own weight of high leverage and excessive debt.

The Wall Street financial industry also rewards their own well. In 2014 the average bonus paid to traders and analysts by the big firms was $172,860. In 1986 the average Wall Street bonus was only $14,120. (McSpadden, 2015)

The leaders of Wall Street's investment firms are also well compensated. In 2014 Mario Gabelli, who manages a number of investment funds earned $88.5 million. Stephen Schwarzman, who is the CEO of the Blackstone Group earned $85.9 million, and Henry Kravis and George Roberts, CEO's of KKR & Co. earned more than $60 million each. (Grocer, 2015)

If the financial industry in the U.S. continues to attempt to create wealth through financial engineering and taking advantage of the general public rather than creating wealth with real investments, we are in danger of repeating the crisis cycle again, as we have many times throughout history, beginning with the Tulip Mania in the Netherlands in the 1630's.

Real wealth is earned and not created with financial engineering, and takes time to earn real returns. Businesses create wealth and economic benefit only if they provide products and services that are beneficial to society, and not through financial engineering.

Business Ethics
Over the past generation there has been an increase in cases of both political and business ethical lapses. Cases of corporate ethical lapses such as Enron, World Com, Arthur Anderson, and Global Crossing are still fresh in the minds of many Americans. All were focused on gaining short-term profits, and driven by management greed, with little or no regard for those who might be harmed. Lapses of personal ethics on the part of individuals include Martha Stewart's insider trading, and most recently the Bernie Madoff Ponzi investment scheme, amongst many others.

Being ethical in conducting business does pay long-term benefits and better corporate financial performance. A recent study conducted by KRW International, found that companies led by moral leaders performed better than those who were not. Unfortunately many corporate leaders do not understand what 'long-run' means as they focus on next quarter's earnings and Wall Street's expectations. (Che, 2015)

The Global Financial Crisis of 2008 is an example of the intersection of greed, extremes of consumerism, and lack of business ethics. It represented a 'perfect storm' that was destined to end with many innocent casualties.

Health Care Ethics

Ethical lapses have not escaped the medical profession and health care industry either. When the Federal Government reduced Medicare payments to health care providers for performing standard procedures, some health care providers began falsifying reports about patient illnesses to claim higher reimbursements. Others refused to treat Medicare patients or treated only the healthier, who would cost less.

To keep insurers from only serving the more healthy patients, the government then agreed to pay more for very sick patients. The higher payments are based on the diagnosis of the doctor, and thereby opens another avenue for fraudulent diagnosis and higher payments to health care providers. (Tozzi, 2015)

Performance Pressures

Pressure for performance often leads to the loosening of ethics and ethical standards and even encouragement and rewards for doing so. Examples include:

- numerous Wall Street scandals aimed at short-term profits and large bonuses
- Georgia school superintendent and teachers changing student test answers to improve test scores and earn bonuses and awards
- Wells Fargo Bank management putting pressure on their employees to increase sales of financial products, which resulted in selling financial products that caused many customers financial distress
- CEO pressures for results and subsequent misstatement of financial results
- LIBOR international interest rate fixing scandal

- high frequency trading systems to profit at the expense of ordinary investors

No profession or industry seems immune to growing cases of unethical behavior.

Automotive Industry

The recent General Motors recall case of faulty ignition switches in millions of cars contributed to the deaths of over 100 people. General Motors engineers and management personnel were aware of the problem many years prior to admission and recall, but did not address it due to concerns over costs. Not until the Federal Government got involved and forced a recall, did GM take proper action.

Another recent case involved faulty automotive air bags manufactured by Takata, a Japanese company. During the U.S. government investigation of the case, it was found that Takata was aware of the deficiencies with the air bags as early as 2007. Between 2009-2011Takata stopped performing global safety audits for financial reasons. The faulty air bags have been linked to 8 deaths and hundreds of injuries. This is the largest recall in the history of the automotive industry, affecting about 32 million vehicles. Takata has supplied millions of air bags to most every automobile manufacturer in the world. (Spector, 2015) (Pfanner, 2015)

Wall Street Ethics

It is now believed by many, that the practices of Wall Street contributed to if not caused the Global Financial Crisis of 2008. The U.S. government thru the SEC (Securities and Exchange Commission) has investigated the practices of many Wall Street firms that make up the heart of our financial system.

As a result of Federal investigations, many of these firms have been prosecuted, found guilty, and charged with billions of dollars in fines. The biggest firms on Wall Street, including Goldman Sachs, JP Morgan Chase, Bank of America, Citigroup, Morgan Stanley, Wells Fargo, and AIG are among the guilty. These are some of the same firms whose unethical practices led to the Global Financial Crisis. Some of these firms also received government bail-out money. Federal fines levied against businesses for unethical practices in 2014 alone amounted to over $87 billion. (Gongloff, 2012)

To date no high level executive of any of these firms has been prosecuted. (Rackoff, 2014)

A more recent scheme on the part of a number of Wall Street firms is what Michael Lewis describes in his book *Flash Boys*. In this book he describes how:

> "...the world's financial markets were designed to maximize the number of collusions between ordinary investors and high-frequency traders-at the expense of ordinary investors and for the benefit of high-frequency traders, exchanges, Wall Street banks, and online brokerage firms." (Lewis, 2014)

In this high speed/high frequency trading scheme, Wall Street firms spent hundreds of millions of dollars to build very high-speed data networks and systems so that they could intercept stock trades before they reached their destination and trade in front of them for their benefit (referred to as front-running.)

100

As an example, if you placed an order to sell a stock, it would be intercepted, and an order to sell would be placed in front of yours. This process often resulted in you receiving less than you would have for your shares. This is one of the many examples where Wall Street works for themselves, and the small guy is often disadvantaged. This practice continues today, as there are no specific regulations against it. It is currently being studied by the SEC.

Ethics and Student Loans

Another area where there has been less than transparent business dealings is student loans. Some college and university financial aid departments have not been completely forth-coming when they convince students to take on ever-increasing amounts of student debt without explaining the long-term impact.

The financial aid departments of a number of higher educational institutions appear to be focused on maximizing the number of students and institutional income, and letting students worry about their debt later.

Many college and university administrations do not appear to accept much responsibility for the amount of debt students take on while attending college and their future ability to repay it. These conditions with student borrowing are similar to the sub-prime mortgage lending prior to the Global Financial Crisis. U.S. colleges and universities are not lending their money, they have no skin in the game, and it is to their benefit to help students borrow as much as is needed for tuition, fees, and other college expenses.

As a consequence of insufficient institutional accountability for student loans, the average student debt for college graduates is now in excess of $33,000, and the default rate is 12-14%. Many students who do not graduate are also saddled with student debt burden.

Offshoring

Offshoring is defined as the transfer of production and services that are performed in the U.S. to other countries. All U.S multi-national companies use offshoring both to reduce costs, and to expand their market reach into foreign countries.

Boeing Offshoring

Boeing is an example of a U.S. multinational corporation that has used offshoring extensively. Boeing is one of two remaining global companies that produce large commercial aircraft. The other is a European company, Airbus.

Boeing sources major components for its latest commercial plane, the Dreamliner 777, from 9 different countries, including Japan, China, France, U.K., Korea, Canada, Sweden, Australia, and Italy. 30% of the content of each plane is sourced from foreign countries. (Plumer, 2013)

Their offshoring strategy allows Boeing to obtain the best price for each major component of the aircraft, and thereby be more competitive in the world aircraft market. It also gives Boeing an advantage in selling aircraft in countries where components are produced. In many countries airlines are government owned. By manufacturing aircraft components in foreign countries,

Boeing is providing jobs in that country. This gives them a negotiating advantage over aircraft companies who do not.

Apple iPhone Offshoring

Another example of extensive offshoring is the production of the Apple iPhone. Apple designs the iPhone, develops the software, and does the marketing in the U.S.

Some of the higher technology components for the iPhone are produced in the U.S., primarily the computer chips and the glass. China, Taiwan, Inner Mongolia, France, Korea, and Italy supply other components, and the majority of the iPhones are assembled in China.

As a result of Apple's offshoring, there are about 700,000 workers in foreign countries (primarily China) producing the iPhone. About 43, 000 Apple employees are in the U.S., and an additional 20,000 Apple employees are located in foreign countries to support overseas production. (VB News, 2015)

Auto Industry Offshoring

The auto industry is a major user of offshoring to lower their costs of production in the U.S. Autos manufactured in the U.S. by GM, Ford, and Chrysler have up to 30% or more of foreign content.

In 2014 auto parts imports totaled $138 billion or $12,135 for every vehicle assembled in the U.S. That is up from $89 billion in 2008 or $10,536 per vehicle. (Shilling, 2015-June)

There are many other examples of products that are 'made in the U.S.' but have a high content of foreign produced materials and components. Products such as construction machinery, machine tools, engines, appliances, and computers all have content that is produced in foreign countries.

Corporate Profits
Since the early 1950's corporate profits have averaged about 6% of GDP. During the recession in 1980 corporate profits dipped to 3% of GDP, but quickly returned to the norm of 6% after the recession.

Beginning around the year 2000, the share of GDP that went to corporate profits began to increase. It steadily grew to about 12%. During the 2008 recession, corporate profits dropped to about 5.5% of GDP, but again quickly recovered. Corporate profits recovered much faster than employment, wages, or the general economy.

In 2013 after tax profits of U.S. corporations were $1.7 trillion or 10% of GDP. In 2012, they were 9.7% of GDP. Before 2012, the highest level of corporate profits by U.S. companies was 9.1% of GDP. That was in 1929, before the stock market crash and the great recession. (Worstall, 2013)

In 2013 the Commerce Department reported that total wages and salaries of all workers in the U.S. was 42.5% of GDP, down from 42.6% in 2012, and lower than any other year since the statistic began. If total compensation of workers, including employer-paid benefits, are included, the share of GDP for workers was 52.7% for 2013, the lowest level since 1948. (Norris, 2014)

Economists are not in agreement as to the reasons why corporate profits are now taking a much bigger slice of the GDP pie. Some economists attribute the increase to increased foreign profits by U.S. corporations which, when held in foreign countries, are not taxed in the U.S. Many U.S. multi-national companies are now earning a higher percentage of their profits from overseas operations than they are earning from their U.S. operations.

In the U.S. there is more offshoring of production, service, and knowledge work, and more layoffs and restructuring of U.S. operations, which also contribute to higher corporate profits. American workers are also experiencing reductions in pay and benefits, which also tend to boost corporate profits.

Foreign investments

As U.S. companies became more global, they increased their investments in foreign countries, and reduced their investments in the U.S.

In 2012 U.S. companies invested $388 billion in foreign countries, while foreign countries invested $166 billion in the U.S. This represents a net outflow of investment from the U.S. of $222 billion. 74% of the foreign investments by U.S. companies were in developed countries such as the U.K., Germany, Canada, and France. 26% were in developing countries such as China, India, Mexico, and Vietnam. (Jackson, 2013)

In 2013 U.S. corporations invested a total of $276 billion in foreign countries and only $159 billion in U.S. operations, for a net outflow of invested capital of $117 billion. (Mataloni, 2014)

Total foreign investment by U.S. companies in foreign countries is now over $3.3 trillion.

Corporate Cash

At the same time that U.S. corporations are investing less in their U.S. operations and more in their foreign operations, the cash that they have available for investments is at an all-time highs. At the end of 2013 U.S. corporations held $1.64 trillion in cash on their balance sheets and another $1.95 trillion in overseas operations. In that year they paid out in dividends $365 billion and used another $565 for stock buy-backs. U.S. corporations have more cash than they ever had, but are choosing to use it to pay higher dividends to shareholders, invest overseas, and buy back shares of their stock to make financial performance look better. Investing in the U.S. does not seem to be one of corporate America's higher priorities today. (Frier, 2014)

Over the ten year period from 2004-2013, the largest 500 U.S. corporations spent $3.4 trillion on stock buybacks, this represented 51% of their net income over this period. (Lazonick, 2015)

The Bottom Line

In the past several decades we have seen a much closer relationship between U.S. corporations and the Federal Government in matters of business interest. This close relationship has resulted in much legislation favoring U.S. businesses, often at the expense of the average American. Millions of dollars spent by corporations and special interest groups have 'bought' much of this corporate influence. The average

American now has little influence on government laws and regulations.

With its focus on growth, profits, and share price, corporate executives have made decisions that are not necessarily in the best long-term interests of employees, suppliers, communities, the environment, government, or the U.S. economy.

For many corporations in America, the principles of stakeholder interests and social responsibility have been supplanted by shareholder interests of maximizing short-term profits.

Corporate executives now receive much more compensation relative to workers, and often unrelated to company performance.

Corporations are now receiving a much larger share of GDP as profits, often at the expense of the American workers and the U.S. government, as many U.S. corporations avoid paying their fair share of corporate income taxes.

In corporate America over the past several decades we have seen:

- a shift in corporate investments from the U.S. to foreign countries
- more offshoring by U.S. corporations, which has contributed to a reduction of jobs for many American workers
- more layoffs, reductions in benefits, and flat wages for many American workers

Driven by a focus on short-term profits, and sometimes by personal greed, there have been many ethical lapses on the part of U.S. corporations, their employees and their leaders. These ethical lapses have damaged the reputation of American businesses, cost many Americans the loss of assets and jobs, and contributed to the Global Financial Crisis.

Corporate America has not consistently worked for the common good of America and Americans for the past several decades. With their close ties to government, corporations have made it much more difficult for the average American to accomplish their goal of a productive and rewarding life for themselves, their families, and future generations.

A recent article in the *MIT Sloan Management Review* summarizes well how U.S. corporate executives and their corporations are not meeting their social responsibility obligations to America and Americans.

> "In his landmark 19th century study of the United States, *Democracy in America*, Alexis de Tocqueville described the genius of American society as 'self-interest rightly understood.' These days, thanks to the mantra of shareholder value and blind belief in the sanctity of markets, we see a great deal of self-interest fatefully, *mis*understood." (Mintzberg, 2015, p. 10)

The challenge to corporate leadership in America is to return to the stakeholder view of their responsibilities, and to fully consider the impact of their decisions on all interested parties, not just shareholders and not just short-term.

U.S. corporate leaders must take a longer term view, and consider the impact on America and Americans first when making major business decisions. We are all Americans first and must work together to preserve our economy and the things that have made America and the free enterprise system successful. It starts with a commitment to America first by U.S. corporations. The 'three-legged stool' needs to stand again for the benefit of all, and not just the business wealthy elite and the politically powerful. We need to restore balance in our American businesses.

Let's now turn to our work, review current trends, and see what has changed and what our opportunities and challenges might be in the future.

Chapter 6
Our Work

The wide-ranging effects of economic globalization and technology are two primary forces that are transforming what most of us do for a living and how we do it.

Technology

Over the past several decades, the rates of technology development and adoption have accelerated. Technology now plays a central role in most every aspects of our lives.

The internet has added new sources of information and capabilities for both businesses and individuals. It has become a platform for many other technological advances such as online commerce, social media, and online education.

Technologies such as drones, driverless cars, robots, nanotechnology, genetically modified foods, global positioning systems (GPS), human genome mapping, bio-medicine, 3-D printing, wireless and broadband communications, LED lighting, alternate sources of energy (solar, geothermal, and wind), sensor technologies, smart phones, hydraulic fracking to extract oil and gas, and artificial intelligence such as the IBM Watson computer, have all been advanced in the past decade, and are having somewhat profound effects on our lives. All of these technologies, and more, are changing the way we live, how we do are work, and what we do to earn a living.

Technology and Jobs

With the technology revolution, jobs in the U.S. are shifting from routine jobs that can be mastered quickly, to more skilled jobs that require thinking and judgment. More employers are using cognitive skills tests before hiring workers to determine if the candidate has the necessary thinking and problem solving skills that today's jobs require. 23% of employers now give some type of skills tests, up from 16% in 2010. (Shilling, 2015)

The use of technology not only affects traditional production jobs but also clerical and other routine office jobs, such as bookkeeping and accounting.

Since 2004, the number of full-time employees in the finance departments of large companies has declined by 40% through a combination of automation and outsourcing. In these large companies, information technology employees declined by 44%, and human resource employees declined by 20%.

Routine legal work is also being impacted by automation and technology. Much of the basic legal research to prepare cases can now be done by 'smart' legal software faster and more thoroughly than a staff of law clerks and lawyers. (Shilling, 2015)

How we earn our living has changed over the past generation, and is projected to change even more dramatically in the next several generations.

Not many years ago, the majority of workers in the U.S. were involved in either directly producing a product, such as steel, cars, phones, home appliances, paper, or televisions, or in supporting these industries.

Now there are robots that do welding and assembly work. Computer controlled machining centers do the work that was once done by highly skilled machinists.

'White-collar' thinking jobs are threatened by technology advances as well. Based on a recent study by Oxford University, about half the middle-class occupations such as trucking, financial advice, optometry, and software engineering will be replaced by technology in the next generation.

Changes in Work

Changes that have taken place in our work and work our environment in the past several decades include:

- Corporate organization structures are flatter with fewer mid-level jobs.
- Information, information sharing, and the availability of information have become an essential part of many jobs, and now includes the use of technologies such as analytics, the internet, GPS, sensor technology, and big data.
- Workers are generally more educated, with about 32% of all workers holding a college degree compared to only 5% in the 1960's.
- With global competition, jobs are generally more time demanding, stressful, and less satisfying for an increasing number of workers.
- Most work places have become more diverse (age, gender, ethnicity, and educational levels).
- More women are participating in the workforce. Today 60% of women are working compared to 43% in 1970.
- Jobs require more teamwork skills, as more companies are adopting a team based approach to work and management.
- More jobs in the U.S. have shifted from manufacturing to service. In 1970 33% of the

workforce was employed in manufacturing; it is now about 9%. Since 2007workers in the service sector increased from 70% to 85% of the total workforce.

- Jobs have become less routine and require more analysis and problem solving skills.
- Real middle class household incomes have been flat for the last decade as the change in our work environment has led to layoffs, restructuring, retraining, and fewer high paying middle-class jobs.

These changes in our workplace and our jobs mean that both different skills and different knowledge are required to successfully participate in the new American workplace. These workplace changes also mean that there is less opportunity for many, even those who are skillful in the new technologies, as the U.S. economy is creating far fewer jobs than available workers with the right skill sets. With the combination of continued technology adaption in the workplace and the effects of economic globalization, this trend is likely to continue for some time.

High Tech Jobs
In spite of the growing use of technology by businesses, there has not been significant job growth in technology jobs in the U.S. According to a recent report by Gary Shilling in his *INSIGHT* newsletter:

> "Most of the new jobs being created are not in high paying manufacturing, information technology or utilities, but in low-paying retailing, and leisure & hospitality...." Since its trough in

February 2010, the leisure & hospitality sector has added 2.2 million jobs. In contrast, employment in the information sector has barely changed..." (Shilling, 2015-June).

Offshoring of Knowledge Jobs
One reason for the lack of growth in the high-tech job sector in the U.S. is the offshoring of knowledge work as well as improvements in productivity in many technology jobs. Improvements in technology such as better programming languages and the use of artificial intelligence, have actually reduced the number of people required to do these jobs.

Several recent studies have been published on offshoring of knowledge jobs. One study suggests that upwards of 30% of technology related knowledge jobs are vulnerable to offshoring.

The decision by many U.S. corporate executives to increase the offshoring of technology and knowledge jobs is driven primarily by lower costs and their desire to not only do production work in foreign countries, but also technology development.

Many U.S. multi-national companies such as IBM, Google, Microsoft, Intel, Oracle, Cisco Systems, Dell Computer, and General Electric have set up operations in foreign countries. These foreign operations are staffed with local technology and knowledge workers. Many are there to support local manufacturing operations.

In many developing countries there is a significant savings in wages by offshoring. An accountant in India earns $5,000 per year, compared to $63,000 for an accountant in the U.S. Most of the higher paying technology and knowledge jobs in the U.S. are much lower paying in many foreign countries.

As many of the developing countries work to improve their educational systems, there will likely be an increase in the number of qualified technical workers in foreign countries competing with American workers in the future.

The technology and knowledge jobs that are most vulnerable to offshoring, include:

Occupation	Annual U.S. Mean Wage
Computer Programmers	$72,010
Electronic Drafters	$51,710
Mechanical Drafters	$46,690
Computer Scientists	$100,640
Actuaries	$95,420
Mathematicians	$90,930
Statisticians	$72,150
Film and video editors	$61,180

(11 Jobs Most Likely to be Outsourced, 2010)

Very few technology and knowledge jobs are immune from offshoring. Most of these jobs can be done in other countries for 20-50% of the cost in the U.S.

U.S. jobs in service industries where physical presence is required are less vulnerable to offshoring. Jobs such as gardening, construction, plumbing, electricians, face-to-face selling, auto mechanics, aircraft maintenance, plumbers, barbers and hair dressers are all less vulnerable to offshoring than most technology and knowledge jobs. Some of these jobs are high paying, but many are not.

In the process of offshoring, U.S. corporations have reduced the number of good paying jobs for Americans. The impact of offshoring by U.S. multi-national corporations was seen during the 2000's, when U.S. multi-national companies cut their U.S. workforces by 2.9 million workers, and increased their overseas employment by 2.4 million. During the 1990's these corporations added 4.4 million jobs in the U.S. and 2.7 million overseas. (Wessel, 2012)

Manufacturing Jobs
Concurrent with the slow growth and offshoring of high-tech jobs in the U.S., we are experiencing a continued decline of manufacturing jobs.

This continuing loss of manufacturing jobs in the U.S. has left many non-college graduates in America with low paying and often part-time jobs.

According to the U.S. Census Bureau, employment in manufacturing in the U.S. peaked in 1979 at 19,553,000 or about 22% of the non-farm workforce. In April of 2015, there were only 12,322,000 Americans (or about 9%) employed in manufacturing. This represents a decline of 37%. During the same period, the population of the U.S. grew from 225 million to 320 million or by 42%.

The loss of manufacturing jobs also correlates with the decline in median household income for those U.S.

households that completed high school but do not hold a college degree.

The median household income for households headed by non-college graduates peaked in 1973 at $56,395 (in constant 2013 dollars). By 2013 it was down to $40,701 or a real decline of $15,694 or 27.8%.

This reduction in the earnings of the non-college graduate households further increases the wage disparity in the U.S. As an example, the U.S. average weekly income for technology and knowledge workers is $1,264 ($65,728 annually), compared to $375 ($19,500 annually) for leisure and hospitality workers.

Part-time Workers
In May of 2015, 4.2% of U.S. workers were working part time, primarily because they could not find full time work. A recent survey shows that there are over 4.5 million Americans who are working part-time, but need and want full time employment to support themselves and their families. This condition of forced part-time workers further reduces household income, and puts more demand on government assistance programs.

There has also been an increase since the 2008 Recession of 'on-demand' or contingent workers.

Contingent Workers
Contingent or on-demand workers are generally defined as those workers who work, not on a regular schedule but only when needed. They either work for themselves, for temporary employment agencies, or for small businesses. Examples of on-demand workers are those

who clean houses, do maintenance work, drive for Uber, do construction work, do gardening, or seasonal farm work.

Of the total current U.S. labor force, 34% or 53 million Americans do some on-demand work. These workers have less dependable incomes, are responsible for their own benefits, and pay self-employment taxes. Most of them are not on-demand workers by choice. Many have been laid off from regular employment and have been unable to find regular full-time jobs.

The General Accounting Office (GAO) most recently reported that contingent workers now account for 40.4% of the total U.S. workforce. The condition of not having sufficient numbers of good paying full time work in the U.S. for all Americans is getting worse, not better.

Routine Jobs
Automation, robotics, artificial intelligence, and other smart technologies continue to replace routine work and workers. Today only 25% of all U.S. employees are in jobs that require routine or repetitive activities. Before the 2008 Recession 35% of workers were in jobs that required routine work.

An example of the continuing loss of jobs that require routine or repetitive work, is at the Port of Los Angeles. They are installing automation that will cut the required number of longshoremen by 50%. These are high paying routine jobs.

Projections are that the number of routine work jobs will continue to drop in the U.S. It is estimated that fully one-third of all jobs in the U.S. will be lost to automation within a decade, and one-half will disappear within two decades.

Middle class workers such as clerks and bookkeepers are also vulnerable to the loss of jobs through technology.

Jobs for individuals who can design and program automated machines and systems, and jobs for service personnel will grow as the U.S .continues to make the transition to the automation of routine work. However, these jobs will not require a large number of workers relative to the total workforce. (Shilling, 2015-June)

Growth of Robotics Industry
In a recent article in *Bloomberg Business*, it was reported that the Japanese have launched a national initiative, referred to as 'The Robotic Revolution', to make significant investments in robotic technology including robotic computing, voice recognition, and machine learning. Their goal is to help Japan offset their aging workforce with robotics so that their standard of living will not be negatively impacted by a shrinking workforce and an aging population.

Japan plans to increase the use of 'intelligent machines' in most industries over the next five years. Japan's plan calls for the expansion of robotic sales from $4.9 billion in 2014 to $12.25 billion by 2020. This represents a two and one-half times increase in robotic production in six years. Japan currently has 50% of the global market for robotics. This will help Japan offset the projected drop in its labor force of 12 percent by 2020.

China, Korea, and the U.S. are also making major investments in robotics. Japan's goal by 2025 is to shave 25 percent off of factory labor costs through the use of robotics and other automation technologies.

Robots are declining in cost to as low as $25,000 each from $100,000 just a few years ago. Small companies can now afford robots. This will lead to a reduction in jobs for small businesses as well. (Bloomberg Business, 2015, pp. 16-17)

According to a recent University of Oxford study, also reported in *Bloomberg Business*:

> "About half of the U.S. jobs are at high risk of being automated, with the middle class being disproportionately squeezed." "Lower income jobs such as gardening or day care don't appeal to robots. But many middle-class occupations such as-trucking, financial advice, optometry, software engineering, have all aroused their interest." (Bloomberg Business, 2015)

Low Paying College Jobs

As the U.S. economy continues to recover from the 2008 recession, more jobs are being created, but they are mostly lower paying and many now require a college degree.

In a recent report in *Barron's,* it was noted that of the 2.5 million jobs created in the past twelve months (from May 2014), 1.9 million or 76% required a college degree. The majority of college level jobs created during this twelve-month period were lower paying jobs in retail, leisure & hospitality, education, and health services. The top-paying industries including finance and mining lost a net of 5,000 jobs during the month of May 2015.

It has been suggested that as a higher percentage of workers earn college degrees, more of the lower paying jobs will require them. Today 38% of those 25 years old or older have a college degree. The law of supply and demand is at work. (Colas, 2015)

In 2014, about half of the recent college graduates worked in jobs that did not require a college degree. As a higher percentage of the U.S. population graduates from college, and globalization and technology continue to affect more knowledge jobs, this trend will likely worsen.

There are many jobs that had not required a college degree in the past but now do, and many college graduates cannot get jobs where they can fully use their education to their advantage. Low paying, low knowledge, low skilled jobs are now requiring a college degree. The U.S. economy is not generating sufficient numbers of jobs where college graduates can fully use their education. The worst of all worlds.

Middle Class Jobs
In his book, *Average is Over,* Tyler Cowen describes how the middle class will be affected as technology and globalization change jobs and the long-term profile of work.
Cowen reports that 60% of the jobs lost during the 2008 Recession were what he refers to as 'mid-wage' jobs, and not the low wage or blue collar jobs that are often

121

related to recessions. 73% of the jobs added to the U.S. economy since the recession were low-wage jobs, defined as jobs paying $13.52 per hour or less. (Cowen, Average is Over, 2013)

The job data suggests that the trend in the U.S. economy of generating a higher percentage of low paying jobs and a smaller percentage of higher paying mid-level jobs is not directly related to the recent financial crisis. This shift to a higher percentage of low-paying jobs has been the trend in the U.S. since 1999. Much of this job trend in the U.S. of generating fewer high-paying mid-level jobs is a result of outsourcing of manufacturing jobs. U.S. companies have also set up operations overseas that are self-sufficient in terms of support staff and technology, replacing these higher paying support jobs in the U.S.

Some economists predict that in the future there will be fewer jobs in the middle-skill range (white collar clerical, administrative and sales). More jobs will be either low skilled and low-paying or high-skill and high-paying. These higher paying job include technical and managerial jobs. Jobs between these two ends are not increasing significantly in number nor in their pay.

In 1982 56% of the jobs in the U.S. were classified as routine, including many traditional office jobs such as bookkeeping, administration, and sales. Today routine jobs make up only 44% of all jobs.

As further indication of the elimination of many of the lower middle class jobs and routine work, in 2013 only

68% of the men between the ages of 30-45 who held a high school diploma were working full time, in 1990 it was 76%.

During the same period, the percentage of knowledge jobs, non-routine, and requiring more cognitive skills, increased from 29% to 38% of all jobs. Non-routine manual jobs increased from 15% to 19% of all jobs. This data clearly shows the shift in work in the U.S. from more knowledge work requiring cognitive skills of a non-routine nature, and to more manual work that is difficult to automate. These appear to be the two extremes of job growth in the U.S. in the future.

U.S. jobs are moving towards a 'barbell' work environment, where there will be a lot of low paying service jobs, fewer jobs in the middle, and jobs that are higher paying but require more cognitive skills. (Rotmam, 2015)

Middle Class Income
Along with the loss of middle-class high paying jobs in the U.S. there has been a shift in the distribution of national income in the U.S. away from workers. In 1990 63% of the total U.S. national income went to workers; by 2011 the percentage had fallen to 58%. Workers are now getting a smaller piece of the economic pie, as corporate profits, corporate executives, shareholders, and government get an increasingly larger share.

In order to maintain their standard of living in light of declining incomes and good paying jobs, about 284,000 U.S. workers have two full-time jobs, and 7.6 million have a part-time job in addition to their full-time employment.

Wages for most workers continue to decline, even after the recession. From 2009 (end of recession) to 2011, the inflation-adjusted median household income dropped by 6.7%, more rapidly than during the recession.

Internet Enabled Jobs
Since the broad-based adoption of the internet, more individuals have started their own businesses. This has given them more control of their own destinies, and an opportunity to use their innovative talents.

Companies such as Facebook, Google, Amazon, Uber, Coursea, Netflix, Match.com, Lyft. Etsy, Airbnb, Priceline, Linked-In, Twitter, and Pay Pal, have all been developed by individuals with an idea coupled with the use of computer technology and the internet. Not only have many new companies emerged, but they have provided Americans with new and different ways to communicate, shop, conduct business, and find information.

Many Americans now sell things on websites such as eBay and Etsy, buy items on Amazon and eBay, and use the Google search engine to get any information they need instantly.

Companies such as Uber and Airbnb are able to offer us work on-demand as drivers, or additional income by renting out a spare room in our home for a day or a weekend. Airbnb is now the world's largest hotel operation in the world with more nightly stays than any other hotel organization. Uber operates in 311 cities in 58 countries and provides over 1 million rides a day. (The Economist, 2015)

The Sharing Economy
The increased use of internet technology and mobile devices such as smart phones has been the basis for a number of entrepreneurial businesses, and the birth of the 'sharing economy', where we can share our resources with others and generate income.

We can share our cars and time with others through participating in internet taxi services such as Uber, Lyft, Sidecar, and Hallo.

We can share our home or apartment by participating in internet based short-term rental services such as Airbnb, Home Away, or Wimdu.

We can share our cooking and meals with others by participating in Eat With or Feastly, where we prepare meals and invite others to join us for a fee.

We can share our property for parking thru the use of Park Whiz, Parking Panda, Spot Hero, or Pango.

We can share or lend money directly to others through Lending Club, Prosper, or Jimubox.

We can also sell our excess electricity generated by renewable sources through Solar City.

We can find odd jobs such as handiwork through Zaarly or Task Rabbit.

We can also buy and sell a variety of items and services directly from and to individuals through any of a number of websites and apps. Craigslist, eBay, Etsy, and many others.

These businesses and many other peer-to-peer businesses are available through the internet and mobile technologies, and link providers and users of goods and services. This creates opportunities for work and additional income for many Americans. (Time, 2015)

Self-employed Workers
A higher percentage of workers in the U.S. are self-employed than in the past several generations. Many self-employed individuals are working as contract employees, while others own and operate his or her own businesses.

There are currently about 15 million self-employed workers in the U.S. Many are self-employed not by choice, but by circumstance. Displaced workers from the Recession of 2008, who could not find regular employment and were forced to look at other options. Many turned to consulting, doing handy-man work, starting a consignment shop, starting an internet business, doing gardening work, providing health-care services, or mowing lawns.

Many self-employed individuals are struggling under the additional burdens of self-employment. Self-employed individuals have to provide 100% of the cost of health and other insurances for themselves and their families, whereas many employers pay the major portion of employee health insurance costs. Self-employed individuals have to pay federal self-employment taxes on their net income, which is twice what they would pay as an employee. Self-employed individuals also have to provide their own retirement plans and fund them with 100% of their own money. Employers typically match a certain percentage of employee contributions to retirement plans. Self-employed individuals do not receive paid vacation, sick days, or family medical leave time. (Clements J. , 2015)

Being self-employed is not all that financially rewarding, and has a lot of risks. The majority of today's self-employed individuals would prefer to be employed full-time in a good paying job.

Job Satisfaction
Current data suggests that most Americans are generally not satisfied with their jobs.

The Conference Board, a New York based non-profit research group, has been conducting annual job satisfaction surveys since 1987.

In their most recent survey in 2014, **52.3%** of the respondents indicated that they **were unhappy with their jobs**.

 In 1987, the year of the first survey, 61.1% had reported being happy with their work, and 38.9% unhappy. The low point of the survey was in 2010 during the recession, when 57.4% indicated that they were not happy with their work.

The survey covers job issues such as security, wages, promotion policy, and benefits. All categories have declined since 1987 except physical working environment and equipment, both of which are seen by employees as better today. (Adams, 2014)

The Bottom Line
In the past several decades, the work that we do, and the skills we need, and how work is done has changed significantly.

Major forces have converged to bring about these changes in work in America: the accelerated development and adoption of automation, information technology, and the internet, and the offshoring of work by American multi-national corporations. Together, the combination of these forces suggest that job growth in the U.S., even for high-paying technology jobs, is likely to fall short of the workforce needs into the future.

Automation, Information, and technology have become the center of an increasing number of U.S. jobs, and this trend is likely to continue.

The ability to understand, develop, use, and troubleshoot and maintain technology, will be essential for many future high paying jobs in the U.S.

Routine work, both physical and mental, is being rapidly transitioned from humans to machines thru automation, robotics, and more intelligent computer knowledge systems.

The American worker will increasingly be faced with global competition for jobs either as a result of offshoring or by competing with foreigners for jobs in America. The American worker will have to continue to be more highly educated and technically trained.

To maximize profits, U.S. multi-national corporations will continue to find the lowest costs for materials, labor, capital, and technology. More of both U.S. manufacturing and knowledge jobs will be lost. Job growth in the U.S., therefore, will likely be lower than required for full and gainful employment for many Americans.

Technology does provide more opportunities for individuals to start new businesses. In total these new businesses are unlikely to have a significant net impact on the overall U.S. economy and employment.

The continued increase in the percentage of Americans with college degrees will likely result in a general decrease in pay for college graduates, especially those with traditional degrees. There is likely to be a continued decrease in the number of high-paying college level jobs, especially in many of the non-technical areas.

In technical fields where there is stronger demand, salaries will likely increase, unless there develops an oversupply. Engineering, the basic sciences, and computer technology along with the traditional fields of medicine are those that appear to offer the best prospects for jobs and good pay for those who pursue a college education.

Good paying jobs will continue to grow in fields of technical support and skilled trades, as these job are required in the U.S. to develop, program, and service equipment and technical systems, as the transition to the use of more technology continues.

Some of the routine work in professions such as accounting, law and medicine is being transitioned to

129

intelligent systems and automation as well, potentially limiting the job growth in these fields.

Many middle class Americans will need to rethink their careers in light of the changes in the nature of work in the U.S.

Let's look at the U.S. educational system and its institutions and see how it is squaring with the changes in work and the challenges faced by our global and technological environments. Without the right education and training, it will become increasingly more difficult in the U.S. to have a good paying job and accomplish ones goals of a happy and fulfilling life.

Chapter 7
Our Educational System

As shown in the previous chapter, the nature of work today has changed. What we do, how we do it, and the skills we need are all much different for the majority of U.S. workers than they were just a few decades ago.

This new work environment requires that our education and training institutions change to prepare students to best meet these new work needs. Institutions of higher education not only have to provide the knowledge and skills needed for today's jobs and careers, but must also do it in a way that is cost-effective and timely.

Many of today's jobs require more technical skills, more problem solving skills, more analysis skills, more critical thinking skills, and more written and verbal communications skills.

We will begin by looking at some of these new work requirements and current issues facing our educational systems. We can thereby determine what the focus of higher education should be to support the needs of the new work environment.

Our discussion and analysis will focus on higher education, as that is where the final phases of career and job preparation are completed. However, to be successful in higher education, students must establish a strong educational foundation which is the domain and shared responsibility of the K-12 educational system, the student, and their parents.

It is a bit late to attempt to develop basic skills in math, English, communications, and the sciences in higher education. Much of the lack of success with students in higher education can be directly attributed to a weak foundation that was not built during the elementary school years.

Focus of Higher Education

In their book, *The Second Machine Age*, Eric Brynjolfsson and Andrew McAfee suggest that our educational system needs to change in order to support the jobs and careers of the future:

> "Curriculums from grammar schools to college-should evolve to focus less on memorizing facts and more on creativity and complex communications. Vocational schools should do a better job fostering problem-solving skills and helping students work alongside robots."
> (Bloomberg Business, 2015)

Of all the countries in the world, Germany has done an effective job in educating and training their workforce for today's and tomorrow's jobs. They have been very successful in matching the needs of the economy with the skills and interests of the student. In this way Germany has been able to continue to be a strong manufacturing economy, and advance into the knowledge economy age.

A Model for Higher Education

As explained in Chapter 6, as the world moves to the use of more sophisticated technology in more of the work that is done, both physical and mental, there will be an increasing need for more workers who understand the mechanical side of technology, such as robots, automated machine tools, and automated systems, so that they can be programed, maintained, and repaired.

In America today, this is an education and training need that is not very well satisfied by our higher educational institutions. It is this educational gap between a full college degree and technical training that needs to be filled.

In the last several decades, higher education and government have focused on getting everyone to have a college degree. With this single-minded focus the very essential technical educational and training needed in today's information and automated work environment has been given short-shift. As a result of pushing everyone to college, we not only have a shortage of technical workers in the U.S, but have a lot of college drop outs, and a lot of college graduates who cannot find college level jobs. Our higher educational system has become out of balance with the needs of our economy as well as society.

Germany has done a very good job keeping up with the hardware software end of technology and the automation of traditional manufacturing jobs as technology has advanced.

In their educational process, Germany separates students into those who want a high-tech production orientated career and those who want a higher knowledge career. They do this through a series of interest, aptitude, and knowledge tests before they graduate from high school.

Those German students who choose high-tech production careers, upon graduation from high school, attend a technical trade school where they are partnered with a local company that fits their career choice. These students serve an apprenticeship as well as attend classes for two to four years, depending on the field of study. Other students who are qualified and interested in a career that requires a four-year college education, pursue that path. College completion rates are much higher in Germany than in the U.S., as are good paying hi-tech manufacturing jobs.

Germany has a very well balanced higher education and training system that is closely aligned with the needs of students, industry, and the entire economy. Students are able to follow either a trade-school track, where they learn both the academic and technical side of their chosen career, or they can follow an academic track, where they focus more on academics.

As a result of Germany's balance education system, even though Germany is not a low-cost labor country such as China, Viet Nam, Bangladesh, or India, it remains a very large and competitive manufacturer. Much of its production is exported. Germany has much higher college success rates than the U.S., where we try to get everyone to go to college, often regardless of desire, need, or ability, with a high percentage dropping out.

In 2014, Germany was the fourth largest exporter in the world, exceeded only by China, the European Union, and the U.S. All of these other countries or regions have much larger populations. German exports include: automobiles, machinery, power generation equipment, and electronic equipment. All are manufactured goods with high labor and technology content.

The German higher education model is a good model that meets the education and training needs of the new information and technology driven workplace.

Japan

In August of 2105 Prime Minister Shinzo Abe of Japan announced a major change of direction in Japan's higher educational system. His plan is to transform all of Japan's government-funded universities to either global leaders in scientific research or vocational training centers. Japan has recognized that higher educational needs have changed and Japan therefore needs to focus their higher education on assuring that today's students are gaining the knowledge and skills needed for tomorrow's jobs. Japan is realigning its educational system to support its future economy, thus helping to assure continued global leadership in technology and employment for Japanese citizens. (Obe, 2015)

More Americans Attending College

The U.S. has experienced a significant increase in the number of students attending college in the last several generations. In 2013 there were 19.5 million Americans attending colleges and universities, in 2003 there were 14.4 million, for an increase over this 10 year period of 35%. The total U.S. population increased by only 10% during this period. (U.S. Census Bureau, 2014)

In 1970 about 11% of U.S. adults held college degrees. Today over 32% hold at least a bachelor's degree. The U.S. economy is not creating enough college level jobs for the supply of college graduates. Many college graduates are working in jobs that do not require a college degree.

Since there is a surplus of college graduates, some jobs that had historically not required a college degree, now do. At the same time, a number of high-paying technical jobs are going unfilled, as there are not enough high school graduates going into many of the technical fields.

In the book, *America's Moment: Creating Opportunity in the Connected Age,* by the Rework America organization, it is pointed out that:

"...Americans need to pay more attention to middle-skilled workers. The global glamour of the Ivy League is perverting the rest of the educational system: universities are so obsessed with rising up the academic ranks, and parents are so preoccupied with making sure that their children get a college education, that the country is devoting too few resources to vocational and technical education. America is crying out for plumbers and technicians, while English literature PhD's cannot get a job." (The Economist, 2015)

Too Many College Graduates
Today about 40% of recent college graduates work in jobs that do not require a college degree. At the same time, a number of high-paying jobs that do not require a full four-year degree, but rather two years of technical training, are going unfilled. Our higher educational system is not supplying enough of the right kinds of

education and training needed for all of the various jobs in the age of technology and knowledge work.

There has been an over-emphasis in the U.S. by government and educational leaders on 'a college education for all', at the expense of not providing a sufficient number of educated and trained workers for many other high paying technical jobs. The U.S. higher educational system is currently out of balance with the needs of today's economy.

Few countries have been able to generate sufficient college level jobs to meet the higher percentage of adults with college degrees. Some of the more successful include:

Country	Percent of College Level Jobs
Luxembourg	59.5%
Singapore	54.7%
Switzerland	51.3%
Israel	49.7%
Iceland	49.2%
Sweden	49.1%
Norway	48.8%
United Kingdom	48.0%
New Zealand	47.2%

The United States ranks number 21 with 42.2% of the economy's jobs requiring a college degree. Many of these jobs had not historically required a college degree, and are lower paying. (McCarthy, 2015)

It is unrealistic to assume that the U.S. economy will create the majority of its jobs to truly require a four-year college degree. No other developed economy has been able to do this, and the U.S. is a much larger than all those who currently have a higher percentage of college-level jobs than the U.S.

Students entering college are often not aware that many good paying jobs do not require a college degree. This situation is creating a greater supply of college graduates than the economy needs. This results in increased competition amongst graduates for college level jobs, and results in students being forced to take jobs that are lower paying.

College Costs
At the same time that enrollment in colleges and universities has increased, the costs of college education have increased as well. The cost of higher education in the U.S. has increased at a rate four times that of inflation over the past few decades.

Because of higher costs, more college students and their parents are forced to borrow money to pay for a college education. This has put most students and many parents in debt. The average debt of a college graduate now exceeds $33,000, and over two-thirds of college graduates have some student debt. About 14% of student loans are currently in default. As a result of student loan debt burden, many students are forced to delay marriage, buying a home, and starting a family. Over 25% of college graduates are forced to move back home and live with their parents after graduation due to the financial burden of student loans and the lack of good paying college level jobs.

Before rushing into a commitment to attend college, students should evaluate their college plans in relation to the potential income and the job opportunities for their chosen career. The potential financial burden of student loans has now become an important consideration in college and career planning for most students.

In 2008 the average annual cost of tuition in the U.S. was about 40% of median family income, up from 25% of median family income in 2000, only an eight-year period.

Due to the increases in the cost of higher education, and the flat to declining real incomes of the middle class, it has become necessary for many students to finance college with debt.

Student loan debt now exceeds $1.2 trillion and is the largest single category of personal debt after home mortgages. Total student debt is now greater than total credit card debt and total auto loans.

At the same time that higher education costs are rising, learning results are declining. Employers are increasingly dissatisfied with the quality of recent college graduates, and their preparedness for careers. The U.S. continues to fall behind the world in educational excellence. Higher education costs are not necessarily resulting in better value or better educational outcomes. (Education, The Chronicle of Higher, 2015)

College Success

According to a recent *Chronicle of Higher Education* report, in May of 2014 only about 55% of those students who started college six years ago had graduated. About 400,000 college students drop out of school each year. Eighteen million undergraduate students were enrolled in U.S. colleges and universities in 2014. This is 50% higher than1990. During the same period the U.S. population grew by 28%. Some estimates are that college enrollment will exceed 20 million by 2023. (Education, Chronicle of Higher, 2015)

Employers of college graduates report an increasing dissatisfaction with the degree of preparedness of college graduates for jobs. Skills such as problem solving, critical thinking, analysis, and communication are most often cited by employers as lacking in current college graduates.

Many of the skills required for job and career success need to be developed at an early age. Communication skills should begin to be developed in elementary school. The ability to think critically, to analyze, and to solve problems should also start to develop at an early age. These skills are going to be more necessary as we move towards a more knowledge, information, and technology based economy.

American leaders and educators need to re-assess the entire educational system to make sure that it meets today's needs, rather than the needs of past generations. America is beginning to fall behind other countries both in educational relevance and excellence.

America Losing Its Edge

As the American higher educational system has become more expensive it has also become less effective in giving students the world-class education they need to compete in today's knowledge, technology, information, and global economy.

Recent reports indicate that on a world-wide comparison, the U.S. college student is not faring well. The U.S. is now 7th in literacy, 27th in math, and 22nd in science. Some of the decline can be attributed to a lessening of standards in U.S. higher education. The current educational system has an overemphasis on testing and not enough emphasis on learning and the development of thinking and reasoning skills. (Harris W. , 2015)

Grade Inflation

With a higher percentage of Americans attending college, one would think that the grades earned on average would decline as more of the less talented and less qualified students join the college ranks. Just the opposite has happened over the past generation.

According to Stuart Rojstaczer, a former Duke University professor, the average GPA at four-year colleges and universities in the U.S. has risen from 2.52 in the 1950s to 3.11 in 2006. (Newelon, 2013)

During the period from the 1960's to 2008, the percentage of 'A's' granted in college went from about 15% of all college grades to about 44%. The percentage of 'C's' granted went from 35% to 15%. The percentage of 'B's' and 'F's' remained essentially unchanged. On the surface, it appears as if the 'C' students of the past are now the 'A' students. The amount of grade inflation varies by higher educational institution, but the trend is undeniable.

As further evidence of grade inflation in U.S. colleges and universities, the average undergraduate GPA for all colleges and universities in the U.S. has increased from 2.93 in 1991 to 3.11 in 2006. In the 1930's the average GPA was 2.35, and in the 1950's the average GPA was 2.52. Grade inflation began to accelerate in the 1980's and continues today. (Healy, 2010)

Grade inflation is a likely contributor to the decline in the quality of higher education in the U.S. More and more employers in the U.S. are increasingly dissatisfied with the preparedness for jobs of recent college graduates, even though students are making better grades.

There is also increasing evidence that grade inflation has contributed to a general decline in student effort as they are less motivated to do their best work. There is now less reward for above average work and additional effort. This corresponds with an overall trend of students spending fewer hours on college course work now as compared to a generation ago.

College average GPA's rose significantly between the 1960's and the 2000's at U.S. colleges and universities. During the same period, time spent studying declined significantly. A study by Phillip Babcock showed that the average study time is about 50% lower for classes where the student expected an 'A' than in classes where the student expected a 'C'. (Babcock, 2010)

In a recent survey of college graduates, 82% self-reported that they cheated in college. Cheating also contributes to the lack of student learning and adequate preparation for jobs and careers.

With the watering down of the standards for a college education, a college degree has less value in the job market, as well it should; and they are easier to get.

College Degree and Income
With the increase in the number of Americans with college degrees, the changes in our work and how we do it, a college degree does not necessarily guarantee a high paying job or career.

Over the ten year period from 2003 to 2013, the only group of college graduates who had a net increase in earnings have been those with advanced post graduate degrees.

Average earnings of those college graduates who held only a bachelor's degree decreased by 8% over the ten year period. Those holding a master's degree saw an average decrease of 7%. Those who held a PhD saw average earnings increase by 4%. Those who held an MD, JD, or MBA saw an average increase of less than 5%.

These income figures represent averages over a range of professions, some have done better and some worse than the average. Technology and some engineering fields have experienced high rates of growth in earnings over the past ten years. The medical profession for some jobs has also done better, as this industry continues to grow and there is still a shortage of some skills.

Our economy is moving more to the use of technology and less use of labor. Routine clerical tasks are also being automated, as many are being done by computers that have much faster and vaster capabilities for both data entry and analysis.

The Bottom Line
In the past several decades, many more Americans have attended and graduated from college. At the same time, the cost of college has increased four times the rate of inflation, forcing 70% of students to borrow money for their education. 40% of the students who start college do not finish.

The number of college level jobs in the U.S. is insufficient to support the number of current graduates. 40% of today's recent college graduates are working in low paying professions or in jobs below their educational level. Some graduates continue on to graduate school in the hopes that they can get a higher paying job with a Master Degree or PhD.

The amount of learning and skill development from a college education has declined in the past two decades, as cheating, grade inflation, reduced academic rigor, and lower student effort has resulted in a lower value of a college education.

More employers have become increasingly dissatisfied with the job readiness of recent college graduates. Skills essential to success in today's work world, such as problem solving, analysis, and communications are found deficient in college graduates by many employers. The U.S. has also fallen behind a number of other countries in the quality of education as measured by learning outcomes and proficiency.

On average, there has been little real growth in the earnings of college graduates over the past ten years. The exceptions have been in technology fields, the medical profession, and other select specialties that require unique skills and where shortages of qualified job candidates exist.

Many higher paying high skilled, technical and support jobs are going unfilled in the U.S. due to the lack of qualified candidates.

A college education for all Americans has not turned out to be the best strategy for our educational system, as it has created an oversupply of poorly educated college graduates and an undersupply of trained technical workers.

An effective higher educational system needs to supply America with the right knowledge, skills, and the right mix needed for the current and future economy, and not yesterday's needs.

American governmental and educational leaders have a lot of work to do to get the current higher, as well as K-12, educational systems aligned to support the new work environment so that the U.S. can be globally competitive, and provide good paying jobs for all Americans.

Chapter 8
Our Life Style and Values

America has changed a lot since I was a young boy growing up in northern Illinois. We have discussed changes in our government, our economy, business, our work, and our education, all of which have been influenced by and have influenced our life style and what is important to us, or our values. It is difficult to determine what influenced what, or to answer the proverbial question, "which came first, the chicken or the egg"?

The reality is that our life-style and values helped to create the world that we now live in. Let's begin by looking at the issue of consumerism, see how that has changed over time, and has influenced and shaped our current society and general way of life.

Consumerism
Today's U.S. economy is primarily based on consumption rather than savings and investment. Today, upwards of 72% of all U.S. economic activity is the personal consumption of goods and services. This is the highest consumption rate of any country in the world, and has been increasing in recent decades. From 1981-2011, personal consumption averaged 67.4% of GDP. (Patton, 2014)

Americans have continued to increase their rate of consumption, even though the real income of the middle class has not increased over the past ten years.

To offset the lack of growth in incomes, many Americans increased their consumer debt or worked more hours or part-time jobs to fuel their growing need to consume.

Personal consumption, having more things and using more services, appears the way many Americans get personal satisfaction from life. Having more has also become a measure of success for many Americans.

When the Global Financial Crisis occurred in 2008, many Americans were forced to cut back on their personal consumption. Many lost their homes, jobs, and much of their wealth, including retirement funds. About $13 trillion of net worth was lost as a result of the crisis.

John Gerzema and Michael D'Antonio, in their book *Spend Shift,* see the financial crisis as perhaps a hopeful beginning of a permanent change in consumerism. They see the potential for Americans to move toward less emphasis on consuming for the sake of having and experiencing, and more on getting more value for what they buy and use.

Gerzema also sees Americans, after the financial crisis, moving toward more meaningful and sustainable values, such as community, volunteerism, durability, environmental impact, and family.

Only time will tell if the recent financial crisis was a turning point away from consumerism or just a necessary temporary pause. Americans have fought for the past several decades to maintain and even increase consumption in the face of falling incomes.

Consumer Debt
Consumer debt declined slightly as a result of the 2008 Global Recession. It caused a slight dip in consumer debt between October 2007 and August 2009, but it has continued its upward trend since then. As of May 2015, total consumer debt, excluding mortgages, was $3.4

trillion. This includes credit card debt (26%), auto and related loans (34%), and student loans (40%). Student loan debt is now over $1.2 trillion. The student loan debt per graduate is now over $33,000. (Money Zine, 2015)

In 1980, average consumer debt per household was $1,540, or 7.3% of average annual household income. By 2013 average consumer debt per household increased to $9,800, or 13.4% of average annual household income.

Auto loans have increased significantly since the financial crisis, as consumers are now paying more for cars. The average price paid for a car in May 2015 was $33,362, up 4.3% from 2014. Consumers are affording higher prices by extending the term of their auto loans. New car loans are now averaging 6.5 years. Not too many years ago the standard auto loan was for 36 months. Some loans are now for 84 months.

Before the Global Financial Crisis in 2008, total household debt was $14 trillion; double the amount it was in 2000 of less than $7 trillion.

With the growth in U.S. consumer debt from 2000 to 2008, we should have seen the financial crisis coming. Since the year 2000, the average inflation adjusted income for the middle class family has declined. Debt was being used to continue high rates of consumption, including new cars, larger homes, more student loans, and many other things that we felt were 'needed' to make our lives more meaningful and fulfilling. (Sufi, 2014)

Increasing levels of consumer debt are a danger to our financial system. When interest rates return to their normal and historical levels, the high level of consumer debt could cause the next financial crisis, as more consumers default on loans due to higher payment requirements. Many Americans have been living beyond their means for several decades and many continue to do so.

In 2015, U.S. consumers are projected to further increase their credit card debt by an additional $55 billion. This will put total credit card debt in the U.S. at its highest level in six years (just prior to the economic crisis). (The Wall Street Journal, 2015, p. B8)

Women Working
Another way many families attempted to maintain their accustomed life style in the face of declining real incomes, is by increasing the number of women in the workforce. Today over 60% of the women of working age are employed, up from 43% in 1970. In many households today, it takes two incomes to meet the basic needs of living. More two family workers has led to many children being raised without adequate parental guidance. (The Economist, 2015)

Lower Cost Alternatives
In the face of falling middle class incomes, many Americans are finding innovative ways to continue to enjoy their current life-style.

Consumers are doing more shopping online, using services such as Uber, rather than taking commercial taxis, using Airbnb to book rooms when traveling, rather than staying in traditional higher cost hotels, using websites like Priceline.com for booking travel, using car-sharing services such as Zipcar, rather than owning a car, and buying more low cost and private label foods, rather than higher cost name brands. Many people are also making more use of public facilities such as libraries, parks, public transportation, and museums.

Home Ownership

Home ownership grew from about 64% of all households in the 1990's to over 69% in 2006. It is now below 64%. Lower incomes, tighter borrowing requirements after the 2008 Financial Crisis, and the lack of consumer savings, have all contributed to the decline in home ownership. Many families are having a difficult time saving for the down payment required and/or meeting the credit score requirements.

Over 5 million American households lost their homes during the Financial Crisis of 2008.

Research has indicated that home ownership helps family stability, and helps keep families together. As an example of how some countries value home ownership, in Ireland home ownership is around 85%. If families get in a situation where they cannot make their mortgage payments, the Irish government provides short-term assistance to keep them in their homes and prevent foreclosure.

An unintended consequence of the decline in home ownership in the U.S. has been an increase in the demand for rental properties, driving up the cost of rent. As of June 2015 rents are up 3.5% over the past year, and wages are up only 2%. This condition puts an increased financial burden on many U.S. households. Median rents in the U.S. now represent 30% of median household income, whereas mortgage payments are only 14.6% of median household income. Since 2008 the number of households in the U.S. renting has increased by over 6 million, and the number of households owning decreased by 2 million. This condition puts additional financial stress on more American families. (Sparshott, 2015)

Self-image
A growing trend in the past decade has been the need to look attractive and youthful no matter how old we are.

In the past several years there has been a significant increase in the use of cosmetic surgery by women. Women now account for 92% of all cosmetic procedures performed.

The U.S. now ranks second in the world in plastic surgeries and accounts for 12.5% of all the plastic surgeries performed in the world; only surpassed by Brazil (the home of the most beautiful women in the world) who accounts for 12.9% of the world's total.

U.S. dermatologists and plastic surgeons have gone from being doctors to being beauticians, performing over 15 million cosmetic procedures in 2014, a 13% increase from 2013. Procedures such as Botox have become very popular, and are even being performed by dentists.

In 2014 U.S. women had 13.6 million cosmetic procedures, including 1.7 million plastic surgeries. Breast augmentation is the top surgical procedure amongst women.

The costs of cosmetic procedures vary by type. $371 for a single Botox treatment, $2,971 for liposuction, $4,509 for a buttock lift, $3,708 for breast augmentation, and $6,550 for a face lift.

As more Americans have cosmetic treatments, and as the U.S. population ages, the cosmetic surgery business is expected to continue to grow and become a more significant part of the health care industry.

Social pressures will continue to be a major driver for the industry's continued growth. If my friends Sally and Jane get face lifts or Botox treatments and they look more attractive, then I need to get one too. (Stein, 2015)

Another industry that has grown as a result of our focus on self and self-expression is the tattoo industry. In the past five years the tattoo industry has grown at an annual rate of 9.8% to annual sales of $722 million in 2014. Americans of all age groups are now getting tattooed in increasing numbers. (World, 2015)

Disability Income
The past generation has seen a dramatic increase in the number of Americans receiving disability income.

In ten years, the number of Americans collecting federal disability benefits grew from 5 million to 8.2 million, a 64% increase. Today there are over 11 million Americans receiving disability income payments. 5% of all Americans between the ages of 25 and 64 are receiving Social Security Disability Income (SSDI). This is double the percent in 1989. Once receiving disability payments, very few leave the program. In 2013 less than 1% of those who were receiving benefits left the program and returned to work. (Phillips, 2015)

The dramatic increase in the number of Americans receiving disability income has occurred at a time when the Occupational Safety and Health Administration (OSHA) and other regulatory agencies have helped make significant improvements in workplace safety. There are also fewer manufacturing jobs which have historically been one of the major sources of disability claims. There are fewer workplace accidents and deaths than ever before, and yet a significant increase in the number and percentage of Americans receiving disability income payments.

The direct cost of disability claims is in excess of $115 billion per year, the equivalent of over $1,500 for every American household.

An audit by the Office of the Inspector General, covering the period from 2003-2013, revealed that 45% of disability recipients were overpaid. This resulted in additional taxpayer costs of almost $17 billion.

The Federal disability program (SSI) currently pays out 25% more in benefits than it receives in taxes, and is projected to be insolvent by 2016. Disability claims increased by 28% when the recession occurred in 2008.

Many disability payments are legitimate and are needed to provide minimal levels of income for those who truly cannot work. Some disabilities are a result of medical conditions such as heart disease, stroke, cancer, complications from diabetes, and mental illness. Individuals who suffer from these conditions need and should have support from this government safety net, as they are unable to provide for themselves. However the trend of increasing numbers of disability payment recipients is an indication that some Americans would prefer not to work, but rather collect government benefits.

Prescriptions Drugs

Over the past generation, America has become a nation on drugs (legal and prescribed drugs, not the illegal ones). Americans of all ages are turning more often to drugs for what ails them, both physically and emotionally. We even use drugs to enhance our physical pleasures such as sex. Viagra, the 'little blue pill' for male erectile dysfunction, and other 'life-style drugs', is now a $5 billion dollar industry in the U.S.

Prescription drug sales in the U.S. in 2009 were $250 billion, and represented over 12% of total health care costs. By 2014, the purchases of prescription drugs had increased by 50% to $374 billion. This was 13% higher than 2013.

Research conducted by the Mayo Clinic showed that almost 70% of all Americans take at least one prescription drug, and more than half take at least two. Antibiotics, antidepressants, and pain relieving opiates were the most common prescriptions taken. The Mayo Clinic survey went on to report that:

"Nearly one in four women ages 50 to 64 were found to be on an antidepressant, with 13 percent of the overall population also on antidepressants."

"Seventeen percent of people in the study were being prescribed antibiotics, and 13 percent were on painkilling opioids." (CBS News, 2013)

Among adults the most common prescription drugs are for cardiovascular disease and high cholesterol according to a report from the CDC in 2014.

This report also showed that the use of prescription drugs has increased dramatically in the U.S. From 2007-2009. The report showed that about 48% of those surveyed reported they were taking prescription drugs compared to 39% in the 1988-1994 period.

About 25% of all children are taking at least one prescription drug. 90% of adults 65 and older are taking prescription drugs. There has also been a fourfold increase in the use of antidepressants among adults. (Thompson, 2014)

> "The U.S. with 5% of the world's population consumes 75% of the world's prescription drugs. 52 million people over the age of 12 have used prescription drugs non-medically in their lives. The number of prescription medicine abusers in 2010 was 8.76 million. Most abused prescription drugs fall under 3 categories:
>
> - **Painkillers:** 5.1 million
> - **Tranquilizers:** 2.2 million
> - **Stimulants:** 1.1 million"
>   (National Institute of Health, 2014)

Prescription drugs are now killing far more people than illegal drugs. Most major causes of preventable deaths are declining, while those from prescription drug use are increasing. An analysis of data recently released from the U.S. Centers for Disease Control and Prevention (CDC) by the *Los Angeles Times* revealed:

155

- For the first time ever in the US, more people were killed by drugs than motor vehicle accidents.
- 37,485 people died from drugs, a rate fueled by overdoses on prescription pain and anxiety medications, versus 36,284 from traffic accidents.
- Drug fatalities more than doubled among teens and young adults between 2000 and 2008, and more than tripled among people aged 50 to 69.

The most commonly abused prescription drugs like OxyContin, Vicodin, Xanax and Soma now cause more deaths than heroin and cocaine combined.(Mercola, 2011)

Americans have become more dependent on prescription drugs of all kinds and for many different purposes. The rate of dependency has increased significantly with the growth of the prescription drug industry.

Dependence on Government
About 50% of all U.S. citizens now receive some form of federal or state government benefits. Many of these benefits are well-earned retirement benefits including Social Security and Medicare. However, many others are ones that were intended by the government to be short-term temporary assistance, but now have become viewed and used as life-time entitlements for many Americans. If this entitlement trend continues, the U.S. is in danger of becoming an entitlement society, and risks losing the spirit of self-sufficiency which has been the foundation of its economic success. Many of the current financial problems in developed countries such as Greece and Spain have been caused by decades of increased dependency on the government. As these

financially distressed countries are learning, it is very difficult to change from a culture of entitlement, once it has grown over generations.

Ethics

In many aspects of their lives, Americans are less ethical than they were several generations ago. Many Americans cheat in some way on their Federal income taxes. We overstate deductions, and do not report all income, such as cash payments and gambling winnings. According to a recent survey, 13% of Americans polled reported that it was OK to cheat on taxes, this is up from 9% in 2009. (Ellis, 2010)

Many Americans claim achievements on resumes not earned, and attempt to embellish their accomplishments to get a job or promotion.

Dishonesty now starts at an early age. In a recent survey of college graduates more than 82% admitted cheating in college. Most of these students started cheating in high school, and many even in grade school.

Some recent examples of personal ethics lapses are Lance Armstrong's use of performance enhancing drugs that helped him win a record seven Tour de France cycling championships.

Other examples include: the steroids scandal in Major League Baseball, the deflating of footballs by the New England Patriots in the 2014 playoff games to give them an edge in getting to the Super Bowl, and the recent accusation that St. Louis Cardinals baseball team hacked into the Houston Astro's data base to get scouting and personal data on players.

157

As a society, Americans seen to be putting more emphasis on winning, not only in sports but in many other aspects of life, including career, business, education, and politics. In order to be successful, we are more often bending or putting aside our core ethical values. If this trend continues, it has the risk of permanently changing America's core values, as today's unethical behaviors become tomorrow's new social norms. This is a socially disturbing trend.

Fraud

Another area of ethical lapse is fraud, which is also illegal. There appears to have been an increase in the amount of fraud. Evidence suggests that both the amount and the scope of fraud has increased. With the explosion of the use of the internet, and the ubiquitous use of other 'smart' devices, it has become easier to retrieve and use personal information in fraudulent ways.

With the use of the internet for filing income tax returns, there has been a significant increase in the number of fraudulent income tax returns filed each year.

In 2014, over 3 million fraudulent income tax returns were filed, costing the Federal Government billions of dollars. It has been estimated that federal income tax fraud will cost the federal government, and its tax payers, $21 billion by 2020. Thousands of individuals are participating in this scheme, not just organized crime.

There has also been an increase in the number of credit card breaches in the past several years, including Target, Home Depot, Neiman Marcus, Michaels, PF Changs, Albertson & Supervalu, UPS, Dairy Queen, Goodwill, JP Morgan Chase, K Mart, Staples, and Sony.

The cost of credit card fraud in the U.S. was $7.1 billion in 2013, an increase of 29% from 2012. (Heggestuen, 2014)

Medical fraud has also been on the rise, involving Medicare and Medicaid claims. This fraud costs American taxpayers $65 billion a year. A recent case involved an oncologist in Michigan who has pleaded guilty of Medicare fraud. He gave hundreds of patients' unnecessary treatments, and received millions of dollars in fraudulent Medicare payments as a result. This fraud made him the highest paid oncologist in 2012. (Dolan M. , 2015)

Another medical related fraud involves the investigation of a Tennessee non-profit cancer organization that allegedly bilked donors out of $187 million. There does not seem to be any individual or organization, including charities, that is immune to fraud. (McWhirter, 2015)

There have also been a number of securities and investment fraud cases, such as the Bernie Madoff Ponzi scheme that resulted in losses totaling several billion dollars involving thousands of individuals.

More Americans seem to be looking for ways to make quick and easy money without working for it. The number of fraudulent schemes has increased significantly with the increased use of the internet and credit. They have both made fraud easier and more difficult to trace.

Shorter Attention Span
Since 2000 the average attention span (defined as the amount of concentrated time on a task without becoming distracted) of Americans has decreased from 12 seconds to 8.25 seconds, or a reduction of over thirty

percent. The attention span of a gold fish is reported to be 9 seconds. (Reserarch, 2015)

The decrease in attention span has been primarily caused by the constant use of mobile devices such as smart phones and tablets, and the increase in other forms of external stimulation, and multi-tasking. A recent study showed that 79% of TV viewers use social media while watching or are engaged in other forms of multi-tasking.

Research is now showing that the heavy use of social media is changing how our brain works and contributing to our shortened attention span. We become addicted to the constant use of social media and the internet and our brain is stimulated to seek more, thus further reducing our attention span. (Vidyarthi, 2011)

In his book *Focus: The Hidden Driver of Excellence*, Daniel Goleman shows that now more than ever, we must learn to sharpen our focus if we are to contend with, let alone thrive in, our increasingly more complex world. Goleman shows from studies in fields as diverse as competitive sports, education, the arts, and business, why focus and longer attention spans are essential to success in all fields. (Goleman, 2013)

It has also been discovered that when attention span is short, it makes perceptions and even relationships shallower and less satisfying. When your attention span is short, whatever you do lacks quality. (Tolle, 2005)

As our attention span shortens, we reduce lose our ability to think critically and effectively problem solve. These skills are some of the most important needed in today's globally competitive and technological world. Research has shown that most real creativity and problem solving takes place when there is strong focus on a single idea or problem.

Constant Contact

With the ubiquitous use of smart phones, Facebooking, texting, Tweeting, and a myriad of other socially enabling technologies, Americans have become a society that has a high need to be in constant contact with 'friends'.

Current research indicates that many of these 'friends' are merely acquaintances, and that most of these connections are often not deep personal ones or true friendships. Many individuals have hundreds and even thousands of 'friends' on Facebook, as an example.

According to a recent Pew Research Center survey on the use of social networking, as of September 2014, 71% of online adults use Facebook, 23% use Twitter, 26% use Instagram, 28% use Pinterest, and 28% use LinkedIn.

Women outnumber men but only slightly in their use of social media. 76% of women are social media users, and 72% of men are.

In terms of age groups, 90% of those between the ages of 18 and 29 who are online use social media. 78% of those between the ages of 30 and 49, 65% of those between the ages of 50 and 64, and 46% of those over 65 use social media. 40% of all mobile phone users use social media on their mobile phones.

52% of all Americans over the age of 12 have a profile on a social media site. 52% of online adults now use multiple social media sites. 24% of teenagers reported that they go online 'constantly' and 92% go online daily. 71% of teens use multiple social media sites.

The Pew Research Center looked at some of the specific uses and benefits of social networks. Survey respondents reported:

- Social networking sites are increasingly being used to keep close social ties.
- The average user has more close ties and is less likely to be socially isolated than the average American.
- Facebook users are more trusting than others and have more close relationships.
- Internet users get more support from their social ties.
- Facebook users are much more politically engaged.

The Pew Center Research Center also looked at the impact of the internet and social media on office workers, and found that:

- 51% said it helped expand the people outside the company they were able to communicate with.
- 39% of online workers reported that the internet allowed them more flexibility in work hours.
- 35% reported that the use of the internet helped to increase the number of hours they worked. (Pew Research Center, 2015)

A business downside from the use of social media by employees is the loss of productivity in the workplace. One report estimated a 1.5% productivity loss; other studies have reported even higher losses. Privacy is also at risk as the information that is posted on social media can be available to anyone. (Jung, 2015)

Some of the social downsides of a pervasive use of social media are:

- leads to avoidance of real emotional connections with people, as social media lacks an emotional context
- can diminish thoughtfulness and understanding
- can reduce family closeness
- can cause distractions and reduce time for other activities
- can lead to overall reduction in real social contact

Single Parent Families
The number of children living in single parent households has doubled since 1960. Today about one-third of the children or 15 million are being raised by single parents. The vast majority are being raised by women. (Andersen, 2013)

A recent report of the status of single parenting, indicates that single motherhood is now becoming the new norm, due in part to the growing trend of children being born outside of marriage. This trend has spread to all socio-economic classes, not just the poor. (Dawn, 2015)

About 40% of all children born in the U.S. are born to unwed mothers. 49% of them have never married, and 51% are divorced. According to the Pew Research Center, in 1960 72% of all adults were married, in 2012 just over half were. (Edwards, 2015)

There are about 12 million single parent families in the U.S., with more than 80% headed by single mothers. 17.4 million children are now raised without a father, and nearly half of these children live below the poverty line.

Single moms now make up 25% of all U.S. households, and single dads make up another 6%. 31% of all households in the U.S. are now headed by a single parent. This has quadrupled since the 1960's. There are currently 9.9 million (83%) single mother families and 1.945 million (17%) single father families with children under 18.

The median income for families led by single mothers in 2013 was about $26,000, which is about one-third of that for married couples with children at $84,000.

Only one third of the single mothers receive any child support from the other parent, and the average for those who do is $430 per month or $5,160 per year. 37.2% of the single mothers over the age of 40 receive some form of government benefit. The poverty rate for single mothers in 2013 was 39.6%, nearly five times the rate for married-couple families.

One third of the single mothers could not provide enough food for themselves and their children. One-third of single parents spend half their income on housing; and 45% receive food stamps.

75% of the homeless families in the U.S. are headed by single women with children.

Children born to unmarried mothers are most likely to grow up in single-parent households, and more than two-thirds receive welfare.

Much research has been done on the effects of single parenting on the children. Research comparing children raised in a two-parent households has confirmed that children of single parents are more likely to:

- drop out of school
- use alcohol and drugs
- have psychotic illnesses
- attempt suicide
- get lower grades in school
- not attend college
- have increased anxiety and aggression
- end up in prison (Kelly, 2015)

The social costs of single parenthood are incalculable when considering not only the financial costs of federal and state welfare programs, but also the costs in human terms of the millions of lives lost that could be contributing members of society, both parents and the children.

The significant increase in single parenting in the U.S. over the past several decades, is causing America an untold financial burden. Most single parents require financial support which could be provided thru employment if they were a member of a two-parent household. Other consequences of raising children in a single parent environment are many of these children become single parents themselves. 85% of the youths in prison grew up in single parent families.

Along with the growth in single-parent families, there has been a reduction in the nuclear family in which multiple generations live in the same household and contribute to the family support. Many seniors, for example, are in nursing homes or become wards of the state, when other family members either are not able to or unwilling to care for them.

Diversity

America is becoming more diverse in both general demographics and in life-style choices.

With the 2015 U.S. Supreme Court decision on the right of same-sex couples to marry, America now has legal national acceptance of equal treatment under the law for same-sex marriage. This is an example of how American society is both becoming more diverse, and beginning to become more accepting of diversity.

As America continues to become a more open and accepting society, issues such as the legalization of marijuana and other social changes are likely to occur. America is becoming much more diverse as a country with a broader array of ethnicities and life styles.

In June of 2015, the number of children who are non-white in the U.S. is now over 50% of all U.S. children. By 2020 Hispanics are projected to overtake African Americans as the largest minority race in the U.S.

America was built on the principle of acceptance of everyone irrespective of ethnicity, religious belief, age, education, profession, philosophy, sexual orientation, life-style, or gender. America has also been the 'Land of Opportunity' for anyone who was willing to work hard for what they wanted to achieve. As America becomes more diverse, it is important for each of us to continue to accept those who might be different than we are. We can learn from others who are not like us; we rarely learn anything new or different from those who are our clones.

We Weigh More

Nearly two-thirds of American adults are overweight or obese. The prevalence of obesity in the U.S. has more than doubled over the past four decades. The average sedentary adult consumes between 500-880 more calories per day than required to maintain body weight. This is equivalent to a weight gain of one and one-half pounds per week without exercise. (Jennifer B. Marks, MD, 2015)

34.9% of the adults in the U.S. are obese; 68.5% are obese or overweight; and nearly 40% of adults ages 40-59 are obese. (Foundation, 2015)

Since 1990, American adults have gained an average of 20 pounds. The average male in the U.S. now weighs 196 pounds, and the average female weighs 160 pounds.

As a result of the increase in the average weight of Americans, many more suffer from diabetes, high blood pressure, back problems, and other weight related issues.

Major causes of America's overweight condition include: an increase in the amount of food eaten, the content of the food eaten (bad calories vs good calories), and the lack of sufficient exercise. Stress and the lack of sufficient sleep often lead to over-eating.

Our life-style and economic status often influence the type and quality of the food that we eat. More meals are consumed in fast-food establishments or other restaurants than are prepared at home. Restaurant meals are often higher in fat and calorie content, and are served in larger portions than meals prepared at home.

Our weight is controlled by the basic relationship between inputs and outputs, modified by a quality factor to account for differences between good calories and bad calories. If we take in too much input, caloric intake from food and drink, relative to our output in the calories we burn, we will gain weight. If we eat too many of the wrong quality of calories (sugars, starches and fats), we will gain weight and risk suffering from life-style diseases.

The U.S. Department of Agriculture (USDA) reports that the average American consumed about 20% more calories in 2000 than in 1983. Americans on average, consume 195 pounds of meat a year compared to 138 pounds in the 1950's. Our consumption of added fats rose 45% since 1970. Fast foods now make up 11% of the average American diet. Research confirms that added sugars from soda and energy drinks are now a contributing factor to overweight and obesity.

Today, Americans are eating more, and more of the wrong kinds of food, and getting less exercise. A recent study showed that only 20% of today's jobs require at least a moderate amount of physical activity. In 1960, 50% of the jobs did. Americans on average burn between 120-140 fewer calories per day than 50 years ago. 80% of Americans do not get enough exercise. (Public Health.org, 2015)

Obesity also affects the young. Today over one in three children between the ages of 2-19 are overweight or obese. The health effects of overweight include:

- **"Diabetes:** Type 2 diabetes was once called adult-onset diabetes. Now with the rise in childhood obesity, there is a

168

dramatic rise in the number of children suffering from type 2 diabetes. Untreated, this can be a life-threatening condition.

- **Asthma:** Extra weight can make it harder to breathe and can inflame the respiratory tract. There is a rise in childhood asthma and children with serious asthma are more likely to be overweight.
- **Heart Failure:** Being overweight makes the heart work harder. Overweight children are more likely to grow up to be overweight adults who develop heart problems."
(Generation, 2015)

The dramatic increase in overweight and obese Americans has led to billions of dollars of additional health care costs to society, as well as to productivity losses. A reduction in the longevity of overweight individuals has also occurred, along with a lessened quality of life for many.

No one, except perhaps those in the food industry, the weight loss, or health care benefit from a heavier America.

Personal Safety
Since the coordinated terrorists attack on the Twin Towers in New York City, the Pentagon in Washington, and the third targeted for the Pentagon (plane crashed in a field in Pennsylvania) on September 11, 2001, many Americans feel less safe. The United States is now in a state of continuous war with primarily Islamic Fundamentalists who believe that it is their duty to destroy Western society.

Since September 11, 2001, there have been a number of terrorists' attacks by various fundamentalists groups in a number of countries around the world. India, the U.K,

France, Nigeria, Iraq, Russia, and Yemen are just a few of those who have suffered from recent terrorist attacks. No region of the world seems immune from such attacks.

On one day, Friday June 26, 2015, there were four separate terrorist attacks on three different continents. In Tunisia a terrorist killed 37 tourists on a beach resort. In Kuwait, an Islamic State, a suicide bomber killed 27 people praying in a mosque. In Somalia, al-Shabaab militants killed a number of peacekeeping soldiers. In France a militant decapitated his boss at a U.S. owned gas plant that he allegedly tried to blow up. (Nissenbraum, 2015)

Not only is our physical safety under constant threat by individuals and groups from outside the U.S., but there have also been a number of recent mass shootings in the U.S. by American citizens.

On June 17, 2015, in Charleston, South Carolina, a lone gunman shot and killed nine individuals and wounded a number of others at a predominately black Methodist Church. The shooter had been with the victims for about an hour in a Bible study service prior to opening fire on them. He appears to be a white supremacist who believes that the African Americans have taken over the U.S. and are destroying its culture. He felt a responsibility to stop them. Many other examples such as Newtown, Aurora, Chattanooga, and Columbine are just a few. The FBI reports that there have been over 200 mass murders since 2006; and now one occurs every two weeks. (Today, 2015)

Personal Information Privacy

Americans are also less safe from having their personal information stolen, including their complete identity. Any information that is stored on any electronic media is particularly vulnerable, such as bank account information, tax return information, email correspondence, physical location information, and any information posted on social media.

Americans are at greater risk today, with the use of digital technology, of having everything that is known about them available to anyone at any time. As we continue to use internet technology and 'smart' devices, there is an increased risk of our loss of privacy.

Even the Federal Government is not immune from hacking and cyber-attacks. In June of 2015, the computer systems of the Federal Office of Personnel Management were hacked and information on over 21 million federal employees was stolen. The information stolen included sensitive information on their family members and details of security clearances. The stolen data included 1.1 million sets of finger prints, and details of every background check that had been conducted since 2000. This data, in the hands of the wrong people, could be a threat to U.S. national security. (Yadron, 2015)

There have been many other hacking episodes such as the Target Corporation loss of credit card information on millions of customers in 2014. No one is safe from hacking of personal data.

Personality

In her book *Quiet,* Susan Cain shows how, over the past generation, America has become more of a society that values personality and outward appearances over reflection, thoughtfulness, and depth of character.

Many more Americans have become more interested and even obsessed with personality, both their own and that of their 'heroes'. Americans are more often seeking someone to look up to and admire, and to more strongly develop a 'personality' by imitating those whom they admire.

As a result of the growing 'cult of personality', Americans spend a lot of money on watching and supporting their heroes, including actors and actresses, sports figures, musicians, business leaders, singers, and other personalities.

An example of the amounts of money that Americans spend to see and support heroes is in athletics.

The recent boxing match between Floyd Mayweather and Manny Paquiao resulted in a payday for Mayweather of $300 million and for Paquiao of $160 million. Revenues came from attendance at the fight, pay-for-view TV, endorsements, and memorabilia sales. This fight was the richest boxing match in history.

A recent *Forbes Magazine* article on money in sports, reported that the top 100 athletes in the world earned a total of $3.2 billion in 2014, up by 17% from 2013.

In the past several decades there has been a significant increase in the overall earnings of athletes and their teams. This has occurred during a period when middle-class American household incomes were stagnant to declining.

In 2014, LeBron James (basketball) earned $64.8 million, Phil Mickelson (golf) $50.8 million, Ben Roethlisberger (football) $48.9 million, Lewis Hamilton (racing) $39.0 million, and Jon Lester (baseball) $34.1 million. These are just some of the higher paid athletes in each sports category.

Sales of tickets to music concerts in the U.S. has grown from $1.7 billion in 2000 to $6.2 billion in 2014 or by 265%. The sales of sports merchandise and memorabilia totaled $13.3 billion in 2014. (Statistica, 2015)

We have become a nation that worships our heroes, and are willing to pay a lot of money to support them. (Forbes, 2015)

The Bottom Line
There is no such thing as the 'Average American', but on average we Americans look like the following in terms of how we live (our life-style) and what is important to us.

On average Americans are:

- working more, with more job stress, and often earning less
- better educated but receiving less financial benefit from education
- less physically fit and more overweight, leading to less energy and more health problems
- focused more on self and self-image and now
- using more prescription drugs and at an increasingly younger age, and becoming

addicted to them at greater rates and earlier ages

- more dependent on government for more of our needs and less self-reliant
- raising more children alone rather than in two-parent households
- spending more on health care, but have shorter longevity than countries that spend much less
- suffering from an increasing number of chronic diseases
- more anxious, and have shorter attention spans, causing us to do less deep thinking
- continuing to consume and live beyond our means, increasing our risk of financial problems and decreasing our financial security
- less secure physically, financially, and less able to protect our privacy
- dropping out of the workforce in greater numbers, forcing fewer to support more

Not every American experiences these conditions, but they are conditions that exist and affect increasing numbers of Americans. All Americans do, however, bear some of the social and economic costs of many of these conditions.

Recent surveys have indicated that many Americans are not satisfied with their lives, including their personal life, their job, business, and government. A 2013 Harris poll found that only one-third of Americans polled were very happy overall. (Harris, 2013)

What can we, as individuals, do to change any of these conditions or our current situation? What personal changes can we make in our own lives to change what we can directly control? Many of the current issues outlined in this chapter are within our own control to change.

What can we as a society or a collective nation do about any of these current conditions?

These are the question that the final chapter of this book will attempt to address. Many of these issues in terms of our life-style and values can be addressed by us as individuals. Other issues such as those involving our government, globalization, the economy, business, or our educational system, will need time and a collective will to change. However, we as individuals can begin to influence these institutions by our own personal actions.

Chapter 9
Our Challenges

Given the current state of the America we live in, what are the challenges that we face and how can we accomplish our goal of a happy and fulfilling life?

My purpose in writing this book is to create an awareness of the current situation and to provide a historical perspective on where we have been as a nation, a society, and an economy, as they are interconnected. What happens in one area, has an impact on the others, and on our personal lives.

Once we have a better understanding of the current situation, we can make more informed decisions to plan our future within the context of how things realistically are and not how we might wish them to be.

Some Americans are generally satisfied with their lives, and are living happy and fulfilling ones. However much evidence presented in this book suggests that this is not the case for many Americans.

Change
Many of the current issues and conditions brought out in this book are ones that we as individuals control and can therefore change. We can change a lot of things on our own without major changes in our government, our businesses, the economy, or the educational system. We can always argue that some personal changes would be easier if the outside world would change or be different than it is. The facts are that we can make our lives better in many respects on our own, and thus make our lives more fulfilling and happier.

To make any kind of a personal change we must:

- be aware of what to change
- be willing to make the change
- know how to make the change
- make a personal commitment to change
- have the perseverance to make the change

With understanding, desire, commitment, and determination, we can change or accomplish most anything. Many of the issues that we are facing today are things that we can change.

- We can lose weight.
- We can consume less.
- We can gain additional knowledge and skills to get a better paying job.
- We can stop buying our children and grandchildren so many gifts, and instead contribute to their education fund.
- We can avoid becoming a single parent by practicing protected safe sex.
- We can stop taking un-necessary medication.
- We can be more ethical and honest in our dealings with others.
- We can pack our lunch rather than buying more expensive and less healthy restaurant food.
- We can start saving as little as a dollar a day.
- We can use our current smart phone rather than buy the latest model.
- We can reduce the amount of time we spend on social media and have a more meaningful conversation with a real friend face-to-face.

- We can pay down our credit card balances and buy only what we can afford.
- We can apply ourselves more in school so that we actually develop the skills we need to be successful in our career, rather than memorize our way through and learn little.
- We can learn to cook and entertain at home rather than going out to eat.
- We can work for a few years and save for college instead of taking out student loans.
- We can attend a technical school to gain the job skills we need for a good paying job, rather than attend a four year college.
- We can get books and movies from the public library rather than buy them.
- We can stop taking the kids to the fast-food restaurant and prepare more meals at home.
- We can drop all those expensive channels on cable or satellite TV.
- We can begin to exercise a little each day.
- We can keep our current car or truck rather than buy the newest model.

We can make these and many other changes on our own, and we can start now. We do not need to wait for others or the larger external systems to change. Everything in our lives that we are willing to change in a positive way can make our life better. Each of us has a lot of control over our own life and its direction. The choice is ours, either to take control, or to continue to be controlled by outside forces.

We alone are not going to change the America we live in, nor will it change in a short period of time. We can change ourselves to adapt to it. We can change and adapt to the world as it now is, so we can better control our life's directions and outcomes to live a more fulfilling and happy life.

More on Personal Change
Personal change is difficult and often uncomfortable. Change takes a personal commitment and persistence, requires sacrifice, and often the courage to be different and go against traditional practices. Let's look at an example of how difficult even a simple change can be.

We all have developed patterns of behavior that make our lives routine and thereby easier. We often do things without thinking about them. As an example, each of us either puts on our left shoe first or our right shoe first. Try reversing the process and see how uncomfortable and unnatural it feels. It will take time and commitment to permanently change even the simple act of how we put on our shoes.

Now let's tackle something more difficult, such as quitting smoking. How difficult would that be? Try not drinking soft drinks with sugar (Coke, Pepsi, Mountain Dew, or Dr. Pepper). Research has shown, that sugar-based drinks can contribute to obesity and diabetes if taken in excess.

Try not having dessert at the end of a meal to reduce sugar and calorie intake. Try starting a moderate exercise program to lose weight and get in better physical condition. Try attending a class to gain additional skills you need to get that better paying job or promotion. Try not using credit cards to reduce your debt. Try giving up that shopping trip to the mall. Try not

179

giving the kids and grandkids all those toys that they get bored with quickly, and instead set up a college fund for them. Start saving $5 per week, by giving up that Starbucks coffee once a week, and start a retirement fund.

All of these minor life-style changes can be difficult if we do not see their value, and do not have the commitment, the discipline, or the perseverance and courage necessary to make them happen. We are in charge of our lives, and need to accept that responsibility. No one is going to change you except you. No one is responsible for you and your behaviors, except you. No one is to blame for you unhappiness except you.

We cannot change the world, but we can change how we live in the world by making personal choices to change our behaviors. We can also choose how we react to things that happen that affect our lives. This is the personal challenge and opportunity that each of us has to build a better life for ourselves, our families, and for future generations.

There are a number of good things that have happened over the last several generations in America which help support a better life and a better future for all of us. There are some not so good things that we can work together to change over a longer period of time.

Our challenge is to understand the difference between what we can control and change on our own, and what we need others to help us change. We can all have a better life if we are willing to first change some of our own detrimental behaviors.

Hopeful Signs

Since the Recession of 2008, many Americans have been forced to rethink their lives, as many have lost their jobs, their homes, or are living on lower incomes. Many Americans have been forced to re-examine their spending and consumption, and rethink what is important to them as they faced having less income and fewer assets.

In their recent book *Spend Shift,* John Gerzema and Michael D'Antonio, present research on the behavior of consumers after the 2008 Recession. They report some significant changes. An increasing number of consumers are separating their wants from their needs, and are considering more carefully what they buy and who they buy from. "Consumers are seeking *better,* instead of more." Their research also indicates that more consumers are also reviving core values such as hard work, thrift, fairness, and honesty. (D'Antonio, 2011)

A survey presented in their book, shows that:

- 63% of the population **disagreed** with the statement: 'I find the more I have the more I want.'
- 84.1% **agreed** with the statement: "These days I feel more in control when I do things myself instead of relying on others to do them for me."
- 64.7% **agreed** with the statement: "Since the recession, I am interested in learning new skills, so I can do more myself and rely less on others."
- 64.8% **agreed** with the statement: "Since the recession, I realize that I am happier with a simpler, more down-to-basics lifestyle."

- 76.1% **agreed** with the statement: "Since the recession, I realize that how many possessions I have does not have much to do with how happy I am."
- 77.9% **disagreed** with the statement: "Money is the best measure of success."
- 65.5% **agreed** with the statement: "I believe my friends and I can change corporate behavior by supporting companies that do the right thing."
- 70.9% **agreed** with the statement: "I make it a point to buy brands from corporations whose values are similar to my own." (D'Antonio, 2011)

When a crisis occurs, we are sometimes forced to change. A crisis can be a catalyst for positive change. The old expression: 'necessity is the mother of invention' may be what is needed for us to begin to make some changes in our personal lives that will make a long-term difference.

With all the pain and suffering from the Global Financial Crisis for many Americans, the good that may come from the crisis is that we may begin some life changes that we have needed to make for some time. If enough Americans band together, they can also influence the larger systems such as business and government to change. These are early and potentially hopeful signs of positive change.

Accepting Reality
One of the realities that we must accept is that the U.S. in not necessarily perfect and the best in every aspect. There is a lot that America can learn from other countries. America is no longer the best at everything, as we once were or thought we were.

A recent report looked at some of the more commonly accepted measures of national greatness such as literacy rates, proficiency in math and science, life-expectancy, household income, and exports. Looking at where the U.S. currently is ranked:

Category	U.S Rank
Literacy	7th
Math proficiency	27th
Science proficiency	22nd
Life expectancy	49th
Infant mortality	178th
Median household income	4th
Labor force	4th
Exports	4th

Based on these measures, the U.S. is not the greatest country in the world. We have in fact lost ground on many of these measures over the past several decades. Unfortunately we do lead the world with the highest number of incarcerations per capita and in defense spending. We spend more on defense than the next 26 countries combined. (Harris, 2015)

Change as an Opportunity
In his book, *Rethinking America,* Hedrick Smith outlines some of the challenges that he sees facing the U.S. and the world. Many of these challenges are the result of changes that have occurred in the world in the past several generations. A number have been unintended consequences of beneficial actions. Smith points out that some current trends that are developing will impact future generations. The rapid growth of the

development and use of an ever increasing array of technologies in all aspects of our lives is just one of many changes that is happening now that will have broad-ranging effects on our lives. Being aware of and seeing the opportunities in these types of changes is essential for each of us to continue to live a fulfilling and happy life.

One of the challenges Smith points out is for us to see the need to change as an opportunity rather than as a threat. We need to determine how each of us can find ways to benefit from the change or minimize the negative impact the change has on our lives. (Conn, 1991)

Middle Class Challenge

Robert Reich, former U.S. Labor Secretary, in his book, *Beyond Outrage,* analyzes the aftermath and causes of the 2008 Global Financial Crisis and the current state of working Americans. He points out that:

> "In the 1960's and the 1970's the wealthiest one percent of Americans got 9-10 percent of our total income. By 2007, that share had more than doubled to 23.5%. Over the same period, the wealthiest one-tenth of 1 percent *tripled* its share."

> ".......over the past three decades the wages of the typical worker have stagnated, averaging only about $280 more a year than thirty years ago, adjusted for inflation. That's less than a 1% gain over more than a third of a century. Since 2001, the median wage has actually dropped." (Reich, Beyond Outrage, 2012, pp. xii-xiii)

The changes that have occurred over the past several generations in the distribution of wealth (the fruits of man's labors), present several challenges for both individuals and our society:

- Can we maintain our current life-style over time with lower real incomes?
- Can we adjust our life-style to be more consistent with our current incomes?
- What can we change or give up?
- What are our opportunities as individuals to increase our real incomes and to be able to afford the life-style we currently have or want?
- Is there a way to effectively transfer wealth or more of the gains from productivity from businesses and the wealthy to the American worker without decreasing investment and or demotivating workers?

Making changes to the current economic and business systems would take a lot of time, and require a major change in the current philosophy of business management, Wall Street, and the government. This is unlikely to occur within the current generation. Therefore, in order for many Americans to continue to survive and prosper under the current system, they need to find ways to either change their life-styles to be more compatible with their incomes, or find ways to increase their incomes, or a combination of both. This is a formidable personal challenge for many Americans.

Changing the System

Besides changing some of our personal behaviors that will help us lead a more fulfilling and happier life, we also need to work together to change the larger systems.

We need to work to change our government to be smaller, less intrusive in our lives, more cost effective, less polarized, and more representative of the interests of all Americans.

We need to change our business and free enterprise system from a short-term profit focus to a long-term focus. Business leaders need to be more ethical, and to consider the needs of all stakeholders and of America not just themselves and shareholders. Corporate America's business leaders need to share more equitably the gains from productivity improvements with employees; and to consider America and Americans first when making major business decisions that affect employees and other stakeholders.

We need to change our educational system to provide Americans with the education and training that is needed for today's jobs. The educational system needs to spend more if its resources on education and less on administration, sports, and infrastructure, and be more rigorous in its educational standards, and education to be more affordable.

The only effective and sustainable way to change the current systems of government, business, and education is to become united as a critical mass of Americans with a clear vision of the changes needed.

Americans who seek fundamental change must be committed and persistent in the pursuit of desired

186

changes. They must be willing to apply the right economic pressure on the current leaders and power centers of government, business, and education. They must be willing to make the necessary sacrifices for the common good. Effective permanent change has never come without sacrifice.

Martin Luther King changed the fundamental rights of African Americans in the U.S. with the civil rights movement in the 1960's. Mahatma Gandhi led the movement to free India from British rule, Cesar Chavez did it in California in the 1970's to get fair wages and fair treatment for migrant farm workers. Nelson Mandela did it in South Africa to rid the country of apartheid practices. The American Colonists did it with the Revolution to free themselves from imposed British rule. In many ways we are now being ruled and allowing ourselves to be enslaved by the dual powers of big government and big business.

It is a reality that all systems: governmental, economic, business, educational, and socio-cultural are interlinked and interdependent. Each is a sub-system of the whole. A change in one will have an impact on the others. We must therefore think through the impact that a change in one subsystem has on other subsystems and the entire system. In this way we can avoid potentially harmful unintended consequences. In the past changes have been make by government or business or education without fully analyzing or understanding the full systems impacts; and therefore unintended negative consequences have often occurred.

Today's World

Today Americans find themselves in a world that is much different than the one I grew up in in the 1960's and 1970's. Some of the major differences are:

1. We live in a **global economic world** where we now compete on a global basis for jobs and the production of goods and services. The lowest bidder wins. The result has been fewer high paying manufacturing jobs in the U.S. and the economic stagnation of the middle class, High paying technical and support jobs are also moving to other countries as corporate leaders in the U.S. continue to invest overseas.

2. In spite of flat to declining middle class incomes, many Americans **have attempted to maintain their standard of living** by putting more women to work, working multiple jobs, saving less, borrowing more, and purchasing more goods from lower cost countries. These actions have collectively reduced our personal financial security, supported the transfer of more production overseas, and increased our dependence on government to provide basic needs. Today over 90% of Americans have lower real incomes than a decade ago.

3. Economic globalization has resulted in the U.S. having a **negative balance of trade** with most foreign countries. As Americans buy more goods from overseas, and U.S. corporations invest more overseas, America transfers more of its wealth to other nations.

4. **Over the past several generations the U.S. Federal Government has grown in size** relative to GDP from 4% to 24%, resulting in less money for consumers, less for long term investments, an increasing national debt, and a government less able to provide for long-term needs such as infrastructure, and research and development.

5. **Our economy has changed from one of producing goods** to providing services. This has resulted in the need for more education for Americans and more retraining of workers, the loss of critical capabilities in the U.S. to produce goods, and an increased dependence on foreign countries for many basic needs (clothing, shoes, electronics, etc.). Much of the product design and manufacturing expertise of the U.S. is now falling behind that of other countries, and is not being renewed, decreasing our self-sufficiency as a nation.

6. **Our business environment has become more globally competitive and more short-term profit orientated.** This results in more investments in foreign countries by U.S. corporations and less in the U.S., increased outsourcing of production and service jobs to lower cost regions of the world, a higher percentage of profits and gains from productivity going to management and shareholders and less to workers, loss of jobs in the U.S., more profits retained overseas and not available for U.S. investment, a widening income inequality (more have-nots), and an increased concentration of wealth.

189

7. **Automation and information technologies** play an increasingly more central role in most types of work, resulting in:
    - the automation of many forms of traditionally unskilled and even high-skilled production work
    - the emergence of a new breed of 'knowledge workers'
    - the elimination of many clerical and semi-skilled jobs
    - the emergence of many new products and services such as the internet, online retailing, smart phones, and search engines, which give us instant access to information
    - an infinite variety of products and services from around the world
    - constant contact with our friends and associates.

This technology and information explosion requires many of us to: learn new skills as more technology is applied to our current work, find new jobs and/or careers, as our work is replaced by technology; and increase our educational level to be able to understand, apply, and take full advantage of and survive in this 'brave new world'.

Many more jobs are projected to be eliminated and/or radically changed in the next generation as technology continues to invade most of what we do. We will need to learn how to work side-by-side with our 'robot or intelligent computer assistant'.

8. With the rapid development and adoption of technology, **our education must change**. Higher paying and growth jobs will increasingly be in technical fields such as engineering, physics, biological sciences, computer sciences, and information technology. There will be fewer jobs in traditional production or professional services, resulting in fewer middle class jobs.

9. **Our life style has changed** significantly in the past several generations.

   - Fewer of us are married and have traditional families.
   - More children are being raised in a single-parent environment.
   - We have become more short-term and consumption oriented and less long-term and savings oriented.
   - We are physically heavier and less active; obesity has increased along with related life-style diseases.
   - We are more dependent on government for basic needs of food, shelter, and health care.
   - More of us are receiving disability income.
   - Fewer of us are working.
   - We are spending more of our time in passive activities and less on physical activities.

- We eat out more and cook less at home.
- We spend more on services and technology (phone, internet, cable TV, smart phones, etc.) and less on basics.
- We borrow more on credit cards, and for student loans and auto loans.
- We spend more than we earn.
- We do not save.
- We are not happy in our work.
- We are less involved in our government and our communities.
- We take more prescription drugs for a variety of purposes and for reasons other than illnesses, and do so at a younger age.
- We are more educated but less prepared for our careers.
- We are less honest and ethical in our behavior.

10. **Some of our core values have changed.** What is important to us now is different than what may have been in the past.

- Thrift, patience, and saving before buying drove many of our spending decisions in the past. If we could not afford to pay for what we wanted, we waited and saved before purchasing. Today we freely use credit for the things that we want (instant gratification).
- We want more and bigger. The average size of the American home has increased by 75% over the past several generations,

192

while the average family size has decreased. The average size of cars has increased as well.

- We are looking for heroes and someone to admire and model our lives after.
- We prefer spectator sports rather than participating.
- We are more interested in creating a 'personality' and an image and spend a lot on looking and feeling good.
- Personal and family relationships have become less permanent, as we divorce frequently, and enter relationships outside of marriage.
- More children are born outside of marriage and raised by single parents.
- We are less religious. Fewer of us attend formal churches on a regular basis, and many who do, attend primarily for social reasons.
- Even though most Americans profess a belief in an afterlife and the temporary nature of their time on earth, many go to extreme measures to extend their lives or the lives of their loved ones for short periods of time and at very high costs to families and society.
- We are less honest and ethical. Over 75% of high school and college students participate in some form of cheating.
- We are less willing to work hard and make sacrifices. We seek short-term gratification and easy money.

- We have become more dependent on drugs, both legal and illegal to give us a short-term good feeling and to escape temporarily from the 'burdens of life'.
- We continue to search for ways to control our environment (the external world we live in) through technology. We look for models that explain not only the behavior of the physical world (physics, chemistry, etc.) but also of the human world (economics, psychology, etc.). We seek the predictable model for everything as we value certainty over uncertainty and risk.

Our challenge with the current state of the America we live in and our life-style, is finding ways to live the life that we want within it, and find ways over the long run to work with others to change what we cannot alone change.

How We Got Here

Previous chapters of this book presented a picture of where we are today in the major systems that impact our lives. We have provided some dimensions to the changes that have occurred in the past several generations to life in America.

It is important to understand how we got to where we are so we can better understand the forces that exist in today's society that are leading us in the current directions.

As a way to summarize what I see as some of the events circumstances that set the current trends in motion, I have identified (in hindsight) some of them (not in order of importance):

1. The **New Deal** under President Franklin Roosevelt and the **Great Society** under President Lyndon Johnson set the foundation that has led to some of the 'entitlement' society mentality that now exists in the U.S. Many of these programs have contributed to the growth in government spending, the extended reach of government in our lives, large budget deficits, and the growing welfare society.

2. The lack of **adequate control over U.S. financial institutions** and the financial industry, gave 'Wall Street' and investors the freedom to create ways to accumulate wealth for their own benefit, and often at the expense of millions of Americans. This lack of adequate regulation and control contributed to the recent Global Financial Crisis, and to the income and wealth disparity in the U.S. 'Wall Street' was allowed to develop risky and speculative investment vehicles and processes for their own benefit. In many cases, little economic value was created, real value was often destroyed, and the U.S. financial system has been weakened as a result.

3. Allowing the **higher educational** system to deteriorate by downgrading academic standards and focusing on growth, athletics, infrastructure building, and administration, has resulted in less real and relevant education and much higher costs. Protecting the status quo through accreditation and tenure, and the availability of more money through student loans and federal grants has sheltered higher education from the need to change. An emphasis on passing tests, student retention, high graduation rates, and high GPA's has replaced primary institutional focus on student understanding, skill development, and real learning.

4. Allowing the **Federal Government** to continue to accumulate debt in times of prosperity and not holding it accountable with the same fiscal responsibility that a household or a business would, has led to a cumulative federal budget debt in excess of 100% of GDP.

5. Not holding **American corporations** accountable for providing good paying jobs for Americans and allowing them to make short-term decisions which focused primarily on profitability, and not on the best long-term interests of America and Americans has resulted in a 'hollowing out' of the U.S. economy and less

196

opportunity for good paying jobs for most Americans.

6.   Allowing **free-trade agreements** that did not adequately protect key industries in the U.S., and not effectively addressing violations, has contributed to increased dependency of the U.S. on foreign countries for many basic goods, the loss of much U.S. manufacturing capability in many industries, and the loss of American self-sufficiency. Free trade agreements needed to be more balanced and rigorously enforced to protect American industry and workers.

7.   Allowing America's **trade deficit** to grow to a negative balance of over $3 trillion, has resulted in the transfer of significant wealth from the U.S. to other countries. This weakens the U.S. financial system and makes the U.S. more dependent on foreign countries for many basic goods.

8.   Allowing the **Federal Government to grow** to the size it has and have its reach so deeply extended into every facet of an American's life increases the financial burden of government on Americans. A large and more expansive Federal Government makes Americans more dependent on government, less self-sufficient, and makes it more difficult to do business in America. The size and

197

reach of government also has created an unmanageable, wasteful, costly and dysfunctional bureaucracy.

9. Not limiting the availability of **credit to consumers**, has allowed Americans to live beyond their means and sets the stage for another financial crisis. It also does not supply adequate savings for retirement or investments, and risks that more Americans will be dependent on government in their later years, and increases the risk of future financial crises.

10. Allowing **lobbying** and unlimited political campaign contributions has led to the government being controlled by wealth, businesses, and other special interest groups at the expense of most other Americans.

11. Not finding a way for the legislative branches of the Federal Government and the Executive branch to **work together for the common good** rather than for their own individual political agendas with little concern for the impact on America, has led to a polarized and ineffective government. This polarization has prevented America from dealing with many real issues facing it. The lack of leadership and commitment to the Common Good with a willingness to give up some of our self-interests, is at the root

of many of the unfavorable conditions that exist in America today.

The American Dream

One of the attractions for many of the early immigrants who came to America was the opportunity to escape from oppressive governmental environments and have an opportunity to provide a better life for themselves and their families. They sought the 'American Dream'.

Millions of immigrants who came to the United States were able, through their hard work and the opportunity that America provided, to build a successful life for themselves and their families. This freedom and opportunity has been the foundation of our country becoming the most successful in the world. Today, many Americans no longer think this true or even possible.

A poll taken by the *New York Times* in 2014, found that only 64% of Americans believed that the American Dream was still possible, and 26% said that is was not possible at all. This is the lowest percentage in the last two decades, and much lower than the 72% who believed that the American Dream was still possible in 2009, the depth of the recent Recession.

In this same *New York Times* poll, respondents said that the biggest obstacle in realizing The American Dream was over-regulation by government that interferes with economic growth. This was pointed out as a bigger problem than too little regulation that may create an unequal distribution of wealth. (Thee-Brenan, 2014)

Momentum

A basic law of physics states that 'a body in motion stays in motion unless disturbed by a larger force'. This law can be applied to the major trends that are causing the current situation in America.

Trends like the growing size and influence of government, the growing income inequality and the shrinking of the middle class, the codependent ties between the Federal Government and business, globalization, the failures in our educational system, and other related trends are now in full motion.

The laws of physics further state that 'a body will stay in motion in its current direction until disturbed by an equal or greater force in another direction'. The current trends in America therefore will likely continue for some time as they have powerful momentum forces behind them. It will therefore require very strong and persistent forces to turn the tide. This is the power of the 'Big Mo', momentum.

To make fundamental changes in the America that we now live in, we will need business, government, the educational system, and all Americans to change and support a new way forward that better assures a continued high level of opportunity and prosperity for all Americans, not just the powerful or privileged. America needs to focus more on the 'common good' and less in self-interests.

What We Need from Business
In the last few decades, the primary focus of many U.S. businesses has been the growth of sales revenues and profits.

Much of the corporate growth in revenues and increased profits has come from investments outside the U.S. Many large U.S. multi-national companies now have more that 50% of their annual revenues and profits from foreign operations.

As U.S. corporations were expanding their sales and investments overseas, they were reducing costs in their U.S. operations through actions such as restricting employee wage growth, reducing employee benefits, hiring more contract and part-time employees, using automation and other technologies to reduce employment, and outsourcing materials and labor to other countries. U.S. corporations were also spending billions of dollars to influence U.S. government legislators to write laws that favored their businesses, with often little concern for the impact on U.S. workers.

These and other actions have resulted in record high profits for U.S. corporations. The share of income that goes to corporate profits, compared to that which goes to employees, is at an all-time high, as is executive compensation.

U.S. corporations now hold $2.1 trillion of profits overseas that could be invested in the U.S. and create American jobs. Much of the cash is being held overseas to avoid paying U.S. income taxes. (Rubin, 2015)

Corporate inversions are also being used by an increasing number of U.S. multi-national companies to further minimize the amount of U.S. taxes they have to pay. An inversion involves a U.S. company acquiring a foreign company or merging with a foreign company and then establishes corporate headquarters in a foreign country, thus avoiding U.S. corporate taxation.

U.S. corporations have also spent billions of dollars in buying back their own stock, which uses cash that could have been invested in plant, equipment, technology, and employees. In the short-term, stock buy-backs improve stock performance and price, as there are fewer shares outstanding and therefore earnings per share rise with the same income. Since Wall Street puts value on corporate earnings per share increases, the stock price likely increases, and since many corporate executives have incentive programs based on earnings per share and stock price, they receive more compensation. In the past decade, U.S. corporations have purchased over $4.0 trillion of their own stock. (Platt, 2015)

With these facts it is clear that many large U.S. multi-national corporations have not been working in the best interests of the American worker or of America for the last several decades, but primarily for the benefit of their corporate executives and shareholders.

U.S. corporate executives must focus more on long-term goals, and the needs of America and the American worker. U.S. corporate executives need to make investments and other decisions that are in the best interests of the U.S. as a whole, and not just what is best for corporate America.

U.S. corporations must see their social responsibility as a whole rather than the narrow view that is sometimes taken by focusing on just one specific issues. Corporate stakeholders not only include the shareholders and corporate executives, but also employees, communities, the environment, governments, and suppliers. All stakeholders must all be considered when making major decisions. An understanding of the interrelationships amongst them is essential in corporate decision making.

Every major corporate decision has an impact on all stakeholders and therefore must be completely and deliberately analyzed with a long-term view in mind.

The U.S. financial industry (Wall Street) needs to move away from its emphasis on 'financial engineering' and short-term 'paper' profits and wealth building. The industry needs to focus on long-term real wealth building through investments that create long term economic value and wealth for all. Sound ethical practices also need to return to the financial industry.

What we Need from Government
We as Americans need to find ways to address the size and reach of our currently bloated and ineffective federal government. The current ideological and power-centered polarization that exists in the Federal Government must be eliminated. We must find ways to rise above individual ideological and personal differences, and be willing to work together through constructive compromise for the common good of America and all of our long-term futures. This is the primary responsibility of the federal government, and they have not delivered on it in the past several decades.

We must change our legal system to reduce the number of laws (fewer), their complexity (simpler and clearer), their overlap (eliminate and combine), enforcement (fair and consistent), and penalties (appropriate and equal for all).

We must focus on crimes that have a harmful effect on our safety and security (both 'blue-collar' and 'white-collar'), and less on the 'petty crimes'. More of our resources need to be put on rehabilitation and less on incarceration.

We must reduce the government debt and restore our economy to operate within its means, and work towards a balanced budget. We must outlaw lobbying and pork-barrel legislation, as it is destroying the basic foundation of our democracy, which was built on equal representation and a voice for all Americans.

We must also manage our free trade negotiations, agreements, policies, and enforcement so that the interests of all stakeholders are upheld and not just those of corporate America. We also must find ways to encourage U.S. corporations to invest in the U.S. and to return foreign profits to the U.S. through more effective tax policies. Tax policy should not be a deterrent to making the right decisions for America's best long-term interest, and is should encourage investment in America.

What We Need from the Educational System
We need more technical training, trade schools, and business apprenticeships to create more high-paying non-college degree jobs that are currently going unfilled in the U.S. We should reduce the number of students who attend college, as many never graduate and many of those who do have limited opportunities to earn a good living in their career major.

We also need to lower higher education costs and have more student and career focus in higher education, and less on administration, facilities, and sports.

We need much more rigor in education so students actually gain the knowledge and skills required for their lives and careers. Education needs to return to the basics of educating where students **earn** grades and degrees. Some students will not make it as they either are not qualified to be in college or are not willing to put forth the effort to succeed. There is nothing wrong with failure as that is how we learn and discover what we can and cannot do well.

Education is a shared responsibility between the educator and the student, but at the end of the day, the student must demonstrate that he has acquired the knowledge and skills required not only to graduate, but is also prepared to begin a successful career. These two goals must become primary for higher education.

Leaders in higher education need to see education as their only goal, and the only true measure of success, not winning sports teams, beautiful campuses, large administrative staffs, strong brands, or luxury dorms. Over the past several decades American higher education as well as K-12, have gotten away from the basics of education and must return if Americas are going to have a chance at living a productive and fulfilling life.

What We Need from all Americans
If we are going to make America a better and more secure place for all Americans, we need to be less consumption oriented, more long-term oriented, more self-sufficient, more personally responsible, less self-orientated, and less dependent on government.

We need to become more self-reliant, heathier, more preventive in our approach to health and health care, less dependent on drugs, less dependent on credit, live within our means, and more willing to work and sacrifice for our future, and work for the common good. These are all changes that we can make on our own, we do not have to wait for others or the government or business or the educational system to change.

What it takes to Change?
Large scale, system-wide changes are very difficult to accomplish, especially when they involves communities, governments, businesses, institutions, or entire cultures.

To make changes in these larger systems, we must start with an understanding and a clear picture of where we are today. The 'now' must always be the starting point for any change. We then need a clear picture of the desired change, where we want to go. Only then can we develop a plan for that change. A Change Plan includes:

- a compelling need for the change
- a strong commitment to the change
- a clear picture of that 'future state'
- a coalition of supporters for the change
- the courage to make the change
- a willingness to make sacrifices for the change
- persistence in working for the change
- the recognition and acceptance that effective change takes a long time

What we find today in America is a condition that is out of balance with the fundamentals of our founding democratic principles. All of our major systems from government to business, education, and our own personal values need to change to assure that our American democracy and the benefits that we all have enjoyed for the past several centuries continues for now and thus for future generations.

Balance

In their book, *Balance-The Economics of Great Powers from Ancient Rome to Modern America,* Glenn Hubbard and Tim Kane show that throughout history, whenever imbalances exist in a society, it sets the stage for eventual collapse of the system when they are not corrected. (Kane, 2013)

We find ourselves in the year 2015 with a number of imbalance conditions:

- The power, size, and reach of our government is out of balance relative to the size of our economy and the principles of democracy.
- The influence that business has on our government is out of balance with the general needs of its citizens and for an effective democracy.
- The share of corporate income that goes to executive compensation and corporate profits is out of balance with the share workers receive for an effective economic system to prosper and survive.
- American's growing dependence on government is out of balance for what is needed for a productive and growing free society based on self-reliance and personal initiative.
- Short-term orientation by government, businesses, and many American citizens is out of balance with the needs for building a long-term sustainable economy and society.
- America's growing dependence on foreign countries to provide the goods and services that

are consumed is out of balance with building a sustainable and growing economy.

Our challenge as individual Americans, and as a nation, is to restore balance so that America can survive and continue to grow as a nation, and avoid self-destruction. Any system that gets too far out of balance sets in motion the forces of self-destruction. If the wheels on your car are out of balance and you continue to drive it without correcting the problem, then the wheels will eventually fall off. This is no different than an economic or social system.

Are we lambs being led to slaughter as we have given up much of our personal initiative and are being led by government, business, and social pressures?

If we accept everything and do not question, challenge, and make our own informed decisions, then we are being led by others. As the Buddha said: '

> Believe nothing, no matter where you read it or who said it, not even if I said it, unless it agrees with your own reason and your own common sense.'

If we think for ourselves and find the way that is best for us, and have the courage of our own convictions, we can live a better life, and help build a better world.

Change in America has occurred gradually, like the frog in water. Many of us did not feel the increasing heat as the water nears its boiling point, when we began to feel some pain.

Some feel many Americans have lost the use of common sense, as they too often accept what they hear, and seek easy answers and a quick fix for problems.

Many people often lack depth in their thinking about what affects them and the consequences of our decisions.

Phillip Howard in his book titled, *The Death of Common Sense*, describes our current governmental systems with its increasing emphasis on more and more complex and intrusive laws, as a replacement for America's ability to make free choices. He shows how laws have become so detailed and specific that there is not room for either judgment or for applying practical common sense.

The Final Bottom Line
I will end with the questions that we started the book with:

1. How do we define happiness for ourselves?
2. What is our purpose in life?
3. How can we find a meaningful and fulfilling life for ourselves and our families?
4. What can we change in our lives starting now in our lifestyle and our values that will improve our lives?
5. What do we need to do to work together over to make changes in our government, our economy, business, and our educational system?

Armed with a better understanding of *The America We Live In* today, how we have arrived here, and the interrelationship of the various systems of government, the global world, technology, business, the educational system, and the economy, we are better prepared to determine what we have to do in order to get what we want from life.

We can begin today to make personal changes in our own lives, and to think about how we can work to change the larger systems that need to be changed. We all want to restore America to the place where anyone can achieve the life they want based on their capabilities and willingness to work.

We can restore the American Dream but it will not be easy or quick. We all have to be up for the challenge and willing to make the sacrifices necessary. For the common good, we must restore our will to win and spirit of cooperation and be willing to compromise.

As President John F. Kennedy said: "Ask not what your country can do for you, but rather what you can do for your country." It may be time for us to turn outward to the common good and less inward towards self.

Let us work together to return to a world of common sense and a long-term focus on the common good. These were the founding principles of America and are the reason why we have been so successful in the past.

The future is in each of our hands, and we are all responsible and accountable for the results. What steps will you take now?

References

The World Bank. (2015, July 2). *Data-GDP Growth*. Retrieved from The World Bank: http://data.worldbank.org/indicator/NY.GDP.MKTP.KD.ZG?order=wbapi_data_value_2014%20wbapi_data_value%20wbapi_data_value-last&sort=asc

11 Jobs Most Likely to be Outsourced. (2010, June 20). Retrieved from The Atlantic: http://www.theatlantic.com/business/archive/2010/06/11-jobs-most-likely-to-be-outsourced/58388/

2012 Statistical Abstract: Labor Force, Employment and Earnings. (2014, May 28). Retrieved from United States Census Bureau: http://www.census.gov/compendia/statab/cats/labor_force_employment_earnings.html

About News. (2015, May 13). *US GDP by Year*. Retrieved from About News: http://useconomy.about.com/od/GDP-by-Year/a/US-GDP-History.htm

Adams, S. (2014, June 20). *Leadership: Most Amerians are Unhappy at Work*. Retrieved from Forbes: http://www.forbes.com/sites/susanadams/2014/06/20/most-americans-are-unhappy-at-work/

Andersen, K. (2013, Jan 4). *USA Life Site Family*. Retrieved from USA Life Site: https://www.lifesitenews.com/news/the-number-of-children-living-in-single-parent-homes-has-nearly-doubled-in

Atkinson, A. (2015). *Inequality: What Can be Done?* Boston: Harvard University Press.

Babcock, P. (2010, October). Real Costs of Nominal Grade Inflation? New Evidence from Student Course Evaluations. *Economic Inquiry*, pp. 983-996.

Bacevich, A. (2008). *The Limits of Power* . New York: Henry Holt and Company.

Bank, T. W. (2015, June 8). *The World Bank Household Consumption Expenditures as % of GDP*. Retrieved from The World Bank: http://data.worldbank.org/indicator/NE.CON.TET C.ZS

Barrett, D. (2015, June 17). FBI Looking Into Foul Play. *The Wall Street Journal* , p. A3.

Batchelor, D. J. (2015, May 14). *Inbound Logistics*. Retrieved from Inbound Logistics: http://www.inboundlogistics.com/cms/article/logistics-its-where-the-jobs-are/

Berkrot, B. (2015, April 14). *U.S. Perscription Drug Use Rose 13% in 2014: IMS Report*. Retrieved from Health: http://www.reuters.com/article/2015/04/14/us-health-spending-medicine-idUSKBN0N508I20150414

Binder, A. S. (2015, May 15). The Mystery of Declining Productivity Growth. *The Wall Street Journal* , p. A13.

Bloomberg Business. (2015, June 1). Japan Unleashes a Robotic Revolution. *Bloomberg Business*, pp. 16-17.

Bloomberg Business. (2015, May 25). Robots vs. the Middle Class. *Bloomberg Business*, p. 14.

Brenner, B. (2015, June 1). Japan Unleashes A Robot Revolution. *Bloomberg Business*, pp. 16-17.

Brill, S. (2015). *America's Bitter Pill*. New York: Random House.

Brown, C. (2008). *Inequality, Consumer Credit and the Savings Puzzle*. Northampton: Edward Elgar Publishing, Inc.

Bureau of Labor Statistics . (2014, April 1). Retrieved from Bureau of Labor Statistics: http://www.bls.gov/news.release/empsit.t17.htm

Bureau, U. C. (2015, April 30). *U.S. International Trade in Goods and Services-Balance of Payments*. Washington: U.S. Census Bureau. Retrieved from https://www.census.gov/foreign-trade/statistics/historical/exhibit_history.pdf

Cain, S. (2012). *Quiet*. New York: Random House.

Cappelli, P. (2015). *Will College Pay Off?* New York: Public Affairs Books.

CBS News. (2013, June 20). *Study Shows 70% of Amerians Take Perscription Drugs*. Retrieved from CBS News: http://www.cbsnews.com/news/study-shows-70-percent-of-americans-take-prescription-drugs/

Chaussee, J. (2015, August 3). New Roads. *Bloomberg Business*, p. 25.

Che, J. (2015, March 26). *Huffpost Business* . Retrieved from Huffington Post.

Chen, T. (2015, July 1). *American Household Debt Statistics*. Retrieved from Nerd Wallet: http://www.nerdwallet.com/blog/credit-card-data/average-credit-card-debt-household/

Clements, J. (2015, June 27). Be Your Own Boss-at a Price. *The Wall Street Jounal* , p. B8.

Clements, S. M. (2015, May 8). How Washington Punishes Small Businesses . *The Wall Street Journal*, p. A15.

Colas, N. (2015, June 15). College Does Pay. Stingily. *Barron's* , p. M17.

Conn, J. H. (1991). *Workplace 2000.* New York: Penguin Books.

Cowen, T. (2011). *The Great Stagnation.* New York: Penguin Group, Inc.

Cowen, T. (2013). *Average is Over.* New York: Penguin Group.

Credit Write Downs. (2012, May 1). *Chart of Day: U.S. Manufacturing Employement 1960-2012.* Retrieved from Credit Write Downs: Finance, Economics, Markets and Technology: https://www.creditwritedowns.com/2012/05/chart-of-the-day-us-manufacturing-unemployment-1960-2012.html

D'Antonio, J. G. (2011). *Spend Shift*. San Francisco: Jossey-Boss.

Dawn. (2015, June 1). *Single Mother Guide*. Retrieved from Single Mother Guide: https://singlemotherguide.com/single-mother-statistics/

Dennis, J. (2014, Sept 14). *The top 10 technologies that are changing the world* . Retrieved from Make use of : http://www.makeuseof.com/tag/top-10-emerging-technologies-changing-world/

Dimicco, D. (2015). *American Made*. New York: Palgrave McMillian.

Division, U. C. (2015). *U.S. Trade in Goods and Services-Balance of Payments (BOP) Basis*. Washington D.C.: U.S. Cencus Bureau.

Doh, F. L. (2015). *International Management-Culture, Strategy, and Behavior-Ninth Edition*. New York: McGraw Hill.

Dolan, E. (2013, Sept 6). *Economic Monitor*. Retrieved from Ed Dolan's Economic Blog: http://www.economonitor.com/dolanecon/2013/09/26/us-corporate-profits-at-all-time-high-as-gdp-growth-holds-at-2-5-percent/

Dolan, M. (2015, July 7). Cancer Doctor's Victims to Testify. *The Wall Street Journal*, p. A5.

Donlan, T. G. (2015, August 3). 50 Years in Denial. *Barron's*, p. 39.

Education, Chronicle of Higher. (2015). *Student Success.* Washington: The Chronicle of Higher Education.

Education, The Chronicle of Higher. (2015). *The Value Equation.* Washington: The Chronicle of Higher Eduction.

Edwards, H. S. (2015, August 3). The Next Socal Security Crisis. *Time*, pp. 48-52.

Ellis, B. (2010, February 1 19). *Are You a Tax Cheat?* . Retrieved from CNN Money: http://money.cnn.com/2010/02/19/news/econo my/tax_cheating/

Forbes. (2015, June 29). Leader Board. *Forbes*, pp. 20-22.

Foundation, R. W. (2015, June 29). *Better Polices for a Healthier America.* Retrieved from The State of Obesity: http://stateofobesity.org/fastfacts/

Frier, S. (2014, March 31). *U.S. Companies Hold Record $1.64 trillion on Balance Sheets.* Retrieved from Bloomberg Business: http://www.bloomberg.com/news/articles/2014- 03-31/apple-leads-u-s-companies-holding- record-1-64-trillion

Generation, A. f. (2015, June 28). *Alliance for a Healthier Generation.* Retrieved from Healthiergeneration.org: https://www.healthiergeneration.org/about_chil dhood_obesity/?gclid=Clex3pTsssYCFYU5aQodL9 4KFg

Global Trends 2025: A transformed World. (2008). Washington: U.S. Government Printing Office .

Globalist, T. (2013, November 21). *Just the Facts-CEO's and the Rest of Us*. Retrieved from The Globalist: http://www.theglobalist.com/just-facts-ceos-rest-us/

Goleman, D. (2013). *Focus: The Hidden Driver of Excellence*. New York: Harper Collins.

Gongloff, M. (2012, September 6). *Huff Post Business*. Retrieved from Huff Post: http://www.huffingtonpost.com/2012/09/06/wall-street-financial-crisis-penalties_n_1858738.html

Gongloff, M. (2014, September 16). *Business : 45 Million Americans Stuck Below the Poverty Line*. Retrieved from Huff Post: http://www.huffingtonpost.com/2014/09/16/poverty-household-income_n_5828974.html

Gradeinflation.com. (2015, June 28). Retrieved from Gradeinflation.com: http://www.gradeinflation.com/

Grocer, S. (2015, July 30). Meet Wall Street's Highest-Paid CEO's. *The Wall Street Journal*, p. C4.

Harris. (2013, May 30). *Happiness Survey*. Retrieved from Harris: http://www.harrisinteractive.com/NewsRoom/HarrisPolls/tabid/447/ctl/ReadCustom%20Default/mid/1508/ArticleId/1200/Default.aspx

Harris, W. (2015, May 17). Can tech jobs replace lost manufacturing? . *The Jonesboro Sun*, p. A4.

Haynie, D. (2014, November 17). *U.S. News and Word Report-Eduction*. Retrieved from U.S. News and

World Report: http://www.usnews.com/education/best-colleges/articles/2014/11/17/number-of-international-college-students-continues-to-climb

Healy, S. R. (2010, March 4). Grading in American Colleges and Universities. *Teachers College Record*, pp. 1-6.

Heggestuen, J. (2014, Maech 5). *Tech*. Retrieved from Business Insider: http://www.businessinsider.com/the-us-accounts-for-over-half-of-global-payment-card-fraud-sai-2014-3

Hook, J. (2015, August 4). Unhappy Voters Shake Up Contest. *The Wall Street Journal*, pp. A1-A4.

Howard, P. K. (1994). *The Death of Common Sense*. New York: Random House.

Ibarra-Caton, K. B. (2013). *Direct Investment Positions for 2012*. Washington D.C. : U.S. Department of Commerce Bureau of Economic Analysis .

Industry GDP. (2012, November 13). Retrieved from Bureau of Economic Analysis: http://www.bea.gov/newsreleases/industry/gdpindustry/2012/gdpind11_rev.htm

Jackson, J. K. (2013). *U.S. Direct Investment Aborad-Trends and Current Issues* . Washington : Congressional Reseach Service .

Jacobs, J. (2005). *Dark Ages Ahead*. New York: Random House.

Jeffery, T. P. (2015, May 12). *7,231000 Lost Jobs: Manufacturing Employment Down from 1979 Peak*. Retrieved from cncnews.com: http://cnsnews.com/news/article/terence-p-jeffrey/7231000-lost-jobs-manufacturing-employment-down-37-1979-peak

Jennifer B. Marks, MD. (2015, June 28). *American Diabetes Association*. Retrieved from American Diabeties Association-Clinical Diabetes: http://clinical.diabetesjournals.org/content/22/1/1.full

Johnson, A. (2013, June 24). *76% of Americans are Living from Paycheck to Paycheck*. Retrieved from CNN Money: http://money.cnn.com/2013/06/24/pf/emergency-savings/

Johnson, L. D. (2012, February 22). *History Lessons: Understanding the Decline in Manufacturing*. Retrieved from Minn Post: https://www.minnpost.com/macro-micro-minnesota/2012/02/history-lessons-understanding-decline-manufacturing

Joseph S. Nye, J. (2015). *Is The American Centrury Over?* Malden: Policy Press.

Joseph S. Nye, J. (2015). *Is The American Century Over?* . Cambridge: P:olity Press.

Jung, B. (2015, June 29). *Chron Small Business*. Retrieved from Chron.com: http://smallbusiness.chron.com/negative-effect-social-media-society-individuals-27617.html

Kane, G. H. (2013). *Balance*. New York: Simon & Schuster.

Kelly, J. (2015, June 29). *Does Single Parenting Affect Children?* . Retrieved from How Stuff Works: http://lifestyle.howstuffworks.com/family/parenting/single-parents/single-parenting-affect-children2.htm/printable

Krugman, P. (1995). Growiing World Trade: Causes and Consequences. *Brookings Papers on Economic Activity 1*, pp. 327-376.

Latanich, G. (2015, June 10). Building an Economic Middle Class. *The Jonesboro Sun*, p. A5.

Lazonick, W. (2015). *Stock Buybacks from retain-and-reinvest to distribute-and-downsize*. Washington: Center for Effective Public Management Brookings Institute.

Lewis, M. (2014). *Flash Boys*. New York: W.W. Norton & Co., Inc. .

Lorin, J. (2015, August 10). Asking Everyone's Rich Uncle to Pay for School. *Bloomberg Business*, pp. 29-30.

Lublin, J. S. (2015, June 25). Parsing the Pay and Performance of Top CEO's . *The Wall Street Journal* , pp. B1-B4.

Mataloni, M. I.-C. (2014, July 1). *Direct Investment Positions for 2013: Country and Industry Detail*. Retrieved from White House.gov: https://www.whitehouse.gov

Mather, M. A. (2008). *Population Bulletin*. Washington: Population Reference Bureau.

Matthews, J. W. (2015, May 1). Priciest Drugs Drive Spending by Medicare. *The Wall Street Jornal*, p. 1 and A5.

McAfee, E. B. (2011). *Race Against the Machine.* Lexington: Erik Brynjolfsson .

McCarthy, N. (2015, June 3). *Stastictica-World's Countires for High Skilled Employment.* Retrieved from Stasticia: http://www.statista.com/chart/3521/high-skilled-employment/

McSpadden, K. (2015, March 11). *Time.* Retrieved from Time: http://time.com/3741667/wall-street-bonuses-wages/

McWhirter, C. (2015, July 8). Cancer Non-profit Investigated by Tennessee. *The Wall Street Jounal* , p. A3.

Mercola, D. (2011, October 26). *Death by Perscription Drugs.* Retrieved from Mercola.com: http://articles.mercola.com/sites/articles/archive/2011/10/26/prescription-drugs-number-one-cause-preventable-death-in-us.aspx

Mintzberg, J. C. (2015, Summer, Vol 56, No. 4). Why Corporate Social Responsibility Isn't a Piece of Cake. *MIT Sloan Management Review*, pp. 8-11.

Mitchell, L. M. (2015, August 10). Clinton Proposes Debt-Free College. *The Wall Street Journal* , p. A4.

Mizruchi, M. (2013). *The Fracturing of the American Corporate Elite.* London: Harvard University Press.

221

Money Zine. (2015, July 21). *Money Zine*. Retrieved from Debt Relief Lawyers: http://www.money-zine.com/financial-planning/debt-consolidation/consumer-debt-statistics/

Murray, C. (2015). *By the People-Rebuilding Liberty Without Permission*. New York: Crown Forum.

NAFSA. (2015, May 14). *NAFSA*. Retrieved from Explore International Education: http://www.nafsa.org/Explore_International_Edu cation/Advocacy_And_Public_Policy/Study_Abr oad/Trends_in_U_S__Study_Abroad/

National Institute of Diabetes and Digestive and Kidney Diseases . (2015, June 29). Retrieved from National Institute of Health: http://www.niddk.nih.gov/health-information/health-statistics/Pages/overweight-obesity-statistics.aspx

National Institute of Health. (2014, January 1). *National Institute of Health on Drug Abuse*. Retrieved from National Instutute of Health: http://www.drugabuse.gov/related-topics/trends-statistics/infographics/popping-pills-prescription-drug-abuse-in-america

Newelon, C. (2013, November 12). *College Grade Inflation: Does 'A' Stand for Average?* Retrieved from USA Today: http://www.usatoday.com/story/news/nation/20 13/11/21/college-grade-inflation-what-does-an-mean/3662003/

Nissenbraum, A. T. (2015, June 27). Terrorits Kill Dozens on 3 Continents. *The Wall Street Journal*, p. A1 and A11.

Norris, F. (2014, April 4). *Corporate Profits Grow and Wages Slide*. Retrieved from New York Times: http://www.nytimes.com/2014/04/05/business/ec onomy/corporate-profits-grow-ever-larger-as-slice-of-economy-as-wages-slide.html?_r=0

Obe, M. (2015, August 3). Japan Rethinks Higher Education. *The Wall Street Journal* , p. A8.

Office of Management and Budget. (2011). *Budget of U.S. Government Fiscal 2011*. Washington : Office of Management and Budget.

Ohlemacher, S. (2015, August 10). Modest Changes could save Social Security. *The Jonesboro Sun*, p. A2.

Olson, M. (1982). *The Rise and Fall of Nations* . New York: Yale University .

OpenSecrets.org. (2015, July 17). *Influence and Lobbying-Top Spenders*. Retrieved from OpenSecrets.org: https://www.opensecrets.org/lobby/top.php?ind exType=s

Paine, T. (1997). *Common Sense Dover Thrift Edition*. New York: Dover Publications, Inc. .

Palazzolo, J. (2015, May 18). After Prison, Landing a Job is Tricky. *The Wall Street Journal* , p. A3.

Patton, M. (2014, December 30). *Historical Look at Components of GDP: 1929-2011*. Retrieved from Forbes: http://www.forbes.com/sites/mikepatton/2014/12/30/a-historical-look-at-the-components-of-u-s-gdp-1929-to-2011/

Pena, R. P. (2012, Feburary 23). *The New York Times Education*. Retrieved from The New York Times: http://www.nytimes.com/2012/02/24/education/census-finds-bachelors-degrees-at-record-level.html?_r=0

Pew Research Center. (2015, Jan 9). *Pew Research Center: Internet, Science and Technology*. Retrieved from Pew Research Center: http://www.pewinternet.org/fact-sheets/social-networking-fact-sheet/

Pfanner, Y. K. (2015, June 26). Takataa CEO Drops Hint an Air-Bag Fund is Coming . *The Wall Street Journal* , p. B3.

Phillips, M. (2015, July 6). The Disability Program Needs Help Itself. *Bloomberg Business* , pp. 14-16.

Pierson, J. (2015). *Shattered Consensus*. New York: Encounter.

Platt, E. (2015, April 14). *U.S.Equities*. Retrieved from Financial Times: http://www.ft.com/cms/s/0/48da55fe-e1f7-11e4-bb7f-00144feab7de.html#axzz3i35kBFpA

Plumer, B. (2013, Jan. 18). *Washington Post*. Retrieved from Washington Post :

http://www.washingtonpost.com/blogs/wonkblo
g/wp/2013/01/18/is-outsourcing-to-blame-for-
boeings-787-woes/

Pocket World Figures 2014 Edition. (2014). London: Profile
Books, Ltd.

Price, C. C. (2015, March 27). *Washington Center for
Equitable Growth*. Retrieved from Washington
Center for Equitable Growth:
http://equitablegrowth.org/news/latest-u-s-
economic-growth-numbers-highlight-corporate-
investment/

Public Health.org. (2015, June 28). *Public Health*.
Retrieved from Public Health.org:
http://www.publichealth.org/public-
awareness/obesity/

Quinones, S. (2015). *Dreamland: The True Tale of
America's Opiate Epidemic*. New York:
Bloomsbury.

Rackoff, J. S. (2014, January 9). *The New York Review of
Books-The Financial Crisis-Why Have no High
Level Executives been Prosecuted*. Retrieved
from The New York Review of Books:
http://www.nybooks.com/articles/archives/2014/
jan/09/financial-crisis-why-no-executive-
prosecutions/

Reich, R. (2000). *The Future of Success*. New York: Alfred
Knopf.

Reich, R. (2010). *After Shock*. New York: Alfred Knopf.

Reich, R. (2012). *Beyond Outrage*. New York: Vintage Books.

Reserarch, S. B. (2015, April 2). *Attention Span Statistics*. Retrieved from Statistic Brain Reserach Institute: http://www.statisticbrain.com/attention-span-statistics/

Rework America. (2015). *America's Moment: Creating Opportunity in the Connected Age*. New York: W.W. Norton Company.

Riedl, B. M. (2010, June 1). *Federal Spending by the Numbers* . Retrieved from The Heritage Foundation: http://www.heritage.org/Research/Reports/2010/06/Federal-Spending-by-the-Numbers-2010

Robinson, D. A. (2012). *Why Nations Fail*. New York: Crown Publishing.

Rotmam, D. (2015, July/August). Who Will Own Robots. *MIT Technology Review*, pp. 26-33.

Rubin, R. (2015, March 3). *U.S. Companies Stashing $2.1 trillion overseas to avoid taxes*. Retrieved from Bloomberg Business: http://www.bloomberg.com/news/articles/2015-03-04/u-s-companies-are-stashing-2-1-trillion-overseas-to-avoid-taxes

Rugy, V. d. (2011, July 11). *Mercatus Center George Mason University*. Retrieved from George Mason University : http://mercatus.org/publication/how-much-federal-spending-borrowed-every-dollar

Saunders, L. (2015, April 10). *20% of Earners Pay 84% of Taxes*. Retrieved from The Wall Street Journal : http://www.wsj.com/articles/top-20-of-earners-pay-84-of-income-tax-1428674384

Schumpter. (2015, June 2015 13). The Washington Wishing Well-The Unstoppable rise in lobbying by American business is bad for business itself. *The Economist*, p. 66.

Shilling, G. (2015). *Economic Research and Investment Strategy Volume XXXI, Number 7*. Springfield: A. Gary Shilling & Co., Inc.

Shilling, G. (2015-June). *Gary Shilling's Insight-Economic Reserach and Investment Strategy Volume XXXI No. 6*. Springfield : A Gary Shilling & Co., Inc. .

Smith, A. (2002). *The Wealh of Nations* . New York: Dover Publications .

Smith, H. (1995). *Rethinking America*. New York: Random House.

Sparshott, J. (2015, July 29). Rising Rents Outpace Wages in Wide Swaths of the U.S. . *The Wall Street Journal* , p. A3.

Spector, M. (2015, June 23). Senate Report Faults Takata for Faulty Air Bags. *The Wall Street Journal*, p. B4.

Spence, G. (1993). *From Freedom to Slavery* . New York: St, Martin's Press.

Starr, P. (2012, Sept 10). *Under Obama 11,327 pages of legislation added*. Retrieved from cbsnews.com:

http://cnsnews.com/news/article/under-obama-11327-pages-federal-regulations-added

Stastica. (2015, May 7). *Stastica*. Retrieved from Stasticia: http://www.statista.com/statistics/264682/worldwide-export-volume-in-the-trade-since-1950/

State of Congresss 2013. (2013, January 1). Retrieved from Measue of America: http://www.measureofamerica.org/113-congress-infographic/

Statistica. (2015). *Concert Ticket Sales*. Retrieved from Statistica : http://www.statista.com/statistics/306065/concert-ticket-sales-revenue-in-north-america/

Stein, J. (2015, June 29). Nip, Tuck or Else. *Time*, pp. 40-48.

Steve Matthews, K. M. (2015, May 10). Owning Your Own Home Is Good for Kids. *Bloomberg Business*, pp. 15-16.

Stiglitz, J. (2015). *The Great Divide*. New York: W. W. Norton & Co. .

Strumpf, M. C. (2015, May 4). Debt Engines Revving Up. *The Wall Street Journal*, pp. C1-C2.

Sufi, A. M. (2014). *House of Debt*. Chicago: University of Chicago Press.

The Economist . (2015, June 20). Jailhouse Nation. *The Economist*, p. 11.

The Economist. (2013, June 2). *The Economist Explains*. Retrieved from The Economist: http://www.economist.com/blogs/economist-explains/2013/06/economist-explains-0

The Economist. (2015, August 1). A new age of espionage. *The Economist*, pp. 53-54.

The Economist. (2015, May 16). Briefing: Ending the debt addiction. *The Economist*, pp. 19-22.

The Economist. (2015, May 9-15). Corporate bribery-The anti-bribary business. *The Economist*, pp. 62-63.

The Economist. (2015, April 25). Fighting the secret plot to make the world richer. *The Economist*, pp. 25-26.

The Economist. (2015, June 6). Inequality: What Can Be Done. *The Economist*, pp. 74-75.

The Economist. (2015, May 30). Made to Measure: Factory Automation. *The Economist*, pp. 3-4.

The Economist. (2015, July 4). Still the Land of Opportunity. *The Economist*, p. 73.

The Economist. (2015, June 20). The right choices. *The Economist*, pp. 23-26.

The Economist. (2015, June 13). Uber-Driving Hard. *The Economist*, pp. 61-62.

The Economist. (2015, July 25). Ways of Seeing. *The Economist*, pp. 21-22.

The U.S. Constitution. (2015, May 20). Retrieved from History: http://www.history.com/topics/constitution

The U.S. Largest Imports. (2015, August 17). Retrieved from The World's Richest Countires: http://www.worldsrichestcountries.com/top_us_imports.html

The Wall Street Journal. (2015, June 13). This Week- Charging Ahead. *The Wall Street Journal*, p. B8.

The World Bank IBRD-IDA. (2015, August 17). Retrieved from The World Bank: http://www.worldsrichestcountries.com/top_us_imports.html

Thee-Brenan, A. R. (2014, December 10). *Many Feel American Dream is Out of Reach, Poll Shows.* Retrieved from New York Times: http://dealbook.nytimes.com/2014/12/10/many-feel-the-american-dream-is-out-of-reach-poll-shows/?_r=0

Thompson, D. (2014, May 14). *Daily Healh Reporter.* Retrieved from WebMD: http://www.webmd.com/news/20140514/prescription-drug-use-continues-to-climb-in-us?page=2

Time. (2015, February 9). Some French Guy Has My Car. *Time*, pp. 34-40.

Tocqueville, A. d. (2009). *Democracy in America.* Boston: Bedford/St. Martins.

Today, U. (2015, July 15). *Behind the Bloodshed.* Retrieved from USA Today: http://www.gannett-cdn.com/GDContent/mass-killings/index.html#explore

Tolle, E. (2005). *A New Earth-Awakening to Your Life's Purpose*. London: Penguin Books Ltd. .

Tozzi, J. (2015, June 29). Giving Doctors a Reason to Look for Problems. *Bloomberg Businessweek*, pp. 32-33.

U.S. Census Bureau. (2014, September 24). *Release No. CB 14-177*. Retrieved from U.S. Census Bureau: http://www.census.gov/newsroom/press-releases/2014/cb14-177.html

U.S. Federal Spending. (2015, May 19). *U.S. Federal Spending Since 1900*. Retrieved from US Gov Spending: http://www.usgovernmentspending.com/federal_spending_chart

United States Census Bureau. (2013, June 18). *2013 Capital Spending Report*. Retrieved from United States Census Bureau-Total Capital Expendures for Companies with Employees by Ind.: http://www.census.gov/econ/aces/report/2013/csr.html

VB News. (2015, July 1). *Venture Beat. com*. Retrieved from VB News: http://venturebeat.com/2013/07/31/iphone-manufacturing-graphic/

Vidyarthi, N. (2011, Dec. 14). *Social Media*. Retrieved from Social Times : http://www.adweek.com/socialtimes/attention-spans-have-dropped-from-12-minutes-to-5-

seconds-how-social-media-is-ruining-our-minds-
infographic/87484

Vogus, C. (2015). *A Current View of Higher Education* .
Jonesboro: Create Space .

Weaver, J. D. (2015, June 16). Anthem-Shifting Market.
The Wall Street Jornal, p. A1 and A6.

Wessel, D. (2012, April 19). *Business: U.S. Corporations Shift
Employment Abroad*. Retrieved from The Wall
Street Journal :
http://www.wsj.com/articles/SB100014240527487
04821704576270783611823972

Whybrow, P. (2015, May 11). This Is Your Brain on Easy
Credit. *The Wall Street Journal*, p. A13.

WikipediA. (2015, June 29). *Economy of the United
States*. Retrieved from WikapediA:
https://en.wikipedia.org/wiki/Economy_of_the_U
nited_States

WikipediA. (2015, July 1). *Lobbying in the United States*.
Retrieved from WikipediA:
https://en.wikipedia.org/wiki/Lobbying_in_the_Un
ited_States#A_growing_billion_dollar_business

Wilson, A. E. (June 2002). *U.S. and Foreign Labor
Productivity-International Comparisons*.
Washington: Monthly Labor Review.

World, I. (2015, March 1). *Tatoo Artists: Market Reserach
in the U.S.* . Retrieved from IBIS World:
http://www.ibisworld.com/industry/tattoo-
artists.html

Worldometers. (2015, May 7). *Worldometers-population*. Retrieved from Worldometers: http://www.worldometers.info/world-population/

World's Richest Countries. (2015, May 13). *Top US Imports*. Retrieved from World's Richest Counties: http://www.worldsrichestcountries.com/top_us_e xports.html

Worstall, T. (2013, May 7). *Why Have Corporate Profits been rising as a Percent of GDP-Globalization* . Retrieved from Forbes : http://www.forbes.com/sites/timworstall/2013/05/ 07/why-have-corporate-profits-been-rising-as-a-percentage-of-gdp-globalisation/

Yadron, D. P. (2015, July 10). Over 21 Million Hit by Attack. *The Wall Street Journal* , p. A2.

CPSIA information can be obtained
at www.ICGtesting.com
Printed in the USA
LVHW040913060819
626690LV00003B/241/P